M000308566

The Aztec Empire

An Enthralling Overview of the History of the Aztecs, Starting with the Settlement in the Valley of Mexico

Free limited time bonus

Stop for a moment. We have a free bonus set up for you. The problem is this: we forget 90% of everything that we read after 7 days. Crazy fact, right? Here's the solution: we've created a printable, 1-page pdf summary for this book that you're reading now. All you have to do to get your free pdf summary is to go to the following website:
https://livetolearn.lpages.co/enthrallinghistory/
Once you do, it will be intuitive. Enjoy, and thank you!

We forget 90% of everything that we've read in 7 days...

Get the free printable pdf summary of the book you've read AND much, much more... shhhh...

Enter Your Most Frequently Used Email to Get Started

DOWNLOAD FREE PDF SUMMARY

© Enthralling History

Contents

Introduction

They saw it! They finally saw it. Right there, in front of them, was an eagle, perched on a cactus, eating a snake. The prophecy was fulfilled! The "people from Aztlan" had found the place where they would settle down after countless years of wandering the barren wastelands.

The year was AD 1325, almost 200 years before the first Europeans set foot on the shores of Mexico. A nomadic tribe called the *Mexica* built their city on a small swampy island, an unlikely location for what would become the capital of a great empire. From unpromising origins, the extraordinary Aztec Empire would soon form and expand into a civilization renown for military skills, market exchange, fascinating culture, and extensive and sophisticated agricultural endeavors. Through conquest and alliances with other powerful city-states, the Aztecs developed a vast, organized, densely populated empire that encompassed much of today's Mexico.

This overview of the Aztec Empire will reveal many of the captivating mysteries of this vast nation. What civilizations existed in the area before the Mexica gained supremacy? Where did the Mexica come from? How did they gain ascendency over other civilizations and form their extensive network of power? What was the mythology and religion of the Aztecs, and how was their art a reflection of their belief system? How was their agricultural and market system distinct from surrounding cultures? How did their social order function?

Aztec Calendar[i]

This comprehensive and detailed guide to the Aztec Empire will answer these questions and many more about this intriguing nation and its culture. It will explain the distinctive features of this great empire, what made it exceptional, and how the Aztec culture has had a lasting impact on the modern world. Readers will gain in-depth insight into who the Aztecs were – not just what they did, but how they lived, what they believed, and how they interacted.

Many books have been written about the Aztec Empire, so why is another one needed? Existing books tend to fall into several categories: some are missing information gleaned from the more recent archaeological finds and scholarly studies, some are dry and dusty and overly academic, some focus only on one aspect of the

Aztec Empire, and some are simplistic and limited in scope – geared for a child audience.

The objective of this book is to provide a well-researched and broad presentation of the Aztec Empire in an easy-to-understand and interesting format that keeps the reader fascinated and engaged. History buffs and those simply curious about the Aztecs will appreciate the depth of information and insight woven into this authoritative work, accompanied by striking illustrations that clarify the narrative and bring the Aztec and other Mesoamerican cultures to life.

This guide is divided into four sections, starting with the primary cultures that existed in the area before the Aztec Empire: the Olmecs and Epi-Olmecs, the Toltecs, and the Chichimeca. We will explore how they flourished, what they were famous for, and who were some of their important leaders. We will consider the factors which led to each civilization collapsing, fading into oblivion, or being assimilated by later cultures.

Part Two, The Rise of the Aztec Civilization, focuses on the rise of the Aztec Empire, diving into the origins of the Aztec people and how they defined themselves. This section explores the mystery of the Aztec's home country: Aztlan, in the Lake of the Moon. We will probe theories regarding where it was located and what the word *Aztlan* means. We will investigate who the Mexica tribe were and how they rose to become the dominant tribe of the Aztecs in early settlements in the Valley of Mexico.

The Mexican coat of arms depicts the Mexica-Aztec legend of the eagle eating a rattlesnake while perched on a cactus.[ii]

And what's this legend about an eagle eating a snake while perched on a prickly pear cactus? What does this symbolize, and how did it lead to founding a capital city in the middle of a swamp?

We will analyze the key elements of the establishment of the Aztec dynasty, how the city-states were organized and connected to each other, and how the Aztecs controlled other Mesoamerican city-states. We will study how the Triple Alliance was formed and what was their successful strategy of conquest.

Part Three, the Spanish Conquest, will explore what happened when the Europeans showed up. How did the Aztecs respond when they first spotted strange ships in the Gulf, like nothing they had ever seen? How did the Spanish conquistador Hernán Cortés cunningly form alliances with the Tlaxcala people, rivals of the Aztecs? This section will probe the events leading up to Emperor Moctezuma being held prisoner in his own palace and the revolt of the Aztecs against the Spaniards following the massacre in the Great Temple.

In this section, we will see how the clash played out between two great empires, formerly divided by a great ocean and unknown to the other. How did the Spaniards organize the siege on

Tenochtitlan, the Aztec capital? What factors led to the fall of the great city and the Spanish invaders gaining the upper hand? We will examine what happened when the Spaniards took control, how the Aztecs and other indigenous people adapted to Spain's rule and a new way of life, as they were pressured to abandon their idols and convert (on the surface, at least) to Catholicism.

Part Four - Art, Culture, & Legacy - reviews the fascinating Aztec culture and their continuing impact, beginning with the Aztec religion and who their gods were. Did they really practice human sacrifice? What were their religious rituals like? We will also examine how their market system worked, analyzing the relationships and trade of the Aztecs with other peoples, as well as their education system. And how did the common people live? We will explore what marriage was like in the Aztec culture and intriguing aspects of family and everyday life.

Did you know the Aztecs had a writing system? Their written communication was a form of art, combining pictograms and ideograms. Art was central to Aztec culture, and in Part Four, we will explore the breathtaking beauty of Aztec architecture, sculptures, mosaics, poetry, ceramics, metalwork, and their exquisite featherwork used to dress warriors, priests, and idols. We will examine how their art and other cultural artifacts were influenced by surrounding groups and how they themselves influenced the area around them – even modern-day Mexico and the rest of Mesoamerica.

Let's step back in time and begin following the fascinating journey of a people of mysterious origins who built a city in a swamp and proceeded to develop the vast and breathtaking Aztec Empire.

PART ONE

BEFORE THE AZTECS

Chapter 1: The Olmecs and the Epi-Olmecs

What do rubber balls, chocolate, colossal heads, *werejaguars* (like a werewolf, but jaguar and human), and a pyramid all have in common? They were all cultural distinctions of the Olmecs, the first major civilization or "mother culture" of Mesoamerica, the region extending from central Mexico down to northern Costa Rica.

Formal agriculture in the Americas, especially the widespread growing of maize (corn), goes back to at least the 4th millennium BC, advancing most rapidly in what is now Mexico and Guatemala, as well as the Andes region of South America. Among these farming cultures, the Olmec civilization emerged around 1600 B.C in the swampy tropical lowlands close to the Gulf of Mexico, to the south and east of what is now Mexico City.

The rich and well-watered soil in this area supported productive farming, which provided food for a dense population, and the Olmec established three settlements overlooking the Coatzacoalcos River. We don't know the original Olmec name, but their chief settlement is known today as San Lorenzo Tenochtitlán, in what is now the state of Veracruz. To avoid getting confused with the different Mexica-Aztec city named Tenochtitlán, we will refer to the Olmec city as just *San Lorenzo*.

Olmec Region[iii].

San Lorenzo, a ceremonial center for surrounding agricultural villages, was built on a manmade plateau of 140 acres, which would have required toiling laborers carrying in tons of earthen fill in baskets. Archeologists were amazed to discover an elaborate drainage system with water-storage cisterns, sophisticated for this time period, even in advanced civilizations on the opposite side of the globe. An engineering masterpiece, the aqueduct of San Lorenzo featured covered water channels formed from basalt, providing fresh water for the citizens.

The settlements flourished over time, and by 1200 BC, San Lorenzo was at its peak. The city proper could have housed 5000, with a possible population of 13,000 in the entire area, the first true city in Mesoamerica. This large population generated a hierarchy, with an elite class ruling the city, skilled artisans carving semi-precious minerals, and laborers for the building projects and for farming crops of corn, sweet potato, beans, squash, and cassava, and growing avocado and cacao trees. These foods provided the core diet of the Olmec, along with domesticated dog (their main source of protein) and fish and wild game.

Some of the jade and obsidian used in carvings came from as far as Guatemala, made possible by trade on the Coatzacoalcos River system. Because of their extensive trade system, the Olmec had a cultural influence on a wider area than where they lived. Olmec artifacts have been found as far north as present-day Mexico City and as far south as Guatemala City. Many aspects of Olmec culture were also passed down to future civilizations, including the Aztec.

Archaeologists discovered a palace in San Lorenzo made of earthen walls and floors with a plaster finish, colored with red ochre, made from the iron oxide hematite. Carved from basalt, 13-foot columns supported the roof of the "red palace." This palace would have housed the ruling elite, while commoners lived on the slopes around the city in "wattle and daub" houses: a framework of wood (wattle) covered with wet earth or clay (daubing).

The word *Olmec* comes from an Aztec word meaning "rubber people," and there's a good reason they were called that! The Panama rubber tree is native to tropical areas of Mexico and Central America. The Olmec harvested the sap from this tree and mixed it with sap from morning glory vines to make it supple, so it could be used to form objects. They would press the rubber sap around stones and make rubber balls. Yes! Rubber balls for ball games. The Olmec invented the first rubber balls!

Rubber balls have also been found in Olmec sacrificial pits, indicating they might have been sacrificed to deities. They might have also used them under heavy objects, to roll them from one place to another, as the Olmec were also known for huge stone figurines that would have needed to be transported somehow.

Altar at La Venta[iv].

Around 900 BC, the city of San Lorenzo declined for unknown reasons, but most likely because rivers in the area changed course during that period. The city would have depended on the rivers for trade and for transporting basalt from the mountains. About the same time, another city emerged as the center of Olmec culture. La Venta, settled around 1200 BC, was about 300 years old at the time of San Lorenzo's decline. It rose to dominance as the leading city of the Olmec and remained so for 500 years.

La Venta was in what is now the Mexican state of Tabasco, about ten miles from the Gulf of Mexico and on the Río Palma, a tributary of the Tonalá River. The city was constructed on an island in the middle of a swamp (a recurring theme of cultures in the area), which may have provided natural protection. La Venta's population grew to perhaps 20,000 people, about twice the size of San Lorenzo.

Archaeological examination reveals several distinct sections within the city of La Venta, with a temple complex at the north end of the site and a great pyramid just south of the temple. Curiously, the city is aligned 8 degrees west of north, with almost identical east and west sides. A great deal of planning went into this city!

The La Venta pyramid was once thought to be the earliest known pyramid of the Americas. However, we now know the Caral civilization in Peru built pyramids predating the Egyptian pyramids by 100 years and the La Venta pyramid by over 1000 years. Could the Peruvians have somehow influenced the Olmec culture? Scholars believe a trading system by raft, extending from Peru to Mexico, existed about 1000 years after the Olmec. They believe this is how civilizations in Mexico suddenly adopted metallurgy around AD 800. It's conceivable that a raft trade could have existed much earlier, in the Olmec era, or at least there may have been an occasional traveler between the two areas. Regardless of where they got the idea, the La Venta pyramid ushered in a trend of pyramid building throughout Mesoamerica by various civilizations following the Olmec.

La Venta pyramid

What did this pyramid of La Venta look like? It was rectangular, with steps at the sides going up to the top. Today, even after thousands of years of erosion, it stands 112 feet in height. About 100,000 cubic meters of clay was used in the construction. Like other American pyramids, it was built of packed clay and faced with stone.

Art was a hallmark of Olmec culture. The Olmec made exceptional carvings in jade (using jadeite jade rather than the nephrite jade used in China). These carvings depicted what is believed to be supernatural creatures, such as the part-human and part-jaguar mythological werejaguar.

Olmec Colossal Head[i]

An astonishing art form distinctive to the Olmec were the colossal heads. These awe-inspiring carvings have been found mostly in San Lorenzo, with some in La Venta and a couple in other settlements. These heads were gigantic – up to 11 feet high! Weighing several tons, they were carved from massive volcanic basalt boulders from Cerro Cintepec in the Tuxtlas mountains, over fifty miles away. Another source of basalt used in the colossal heads was the San Martin Volcano.

How did the Olmec move these enormous stones over all those miles? The mysterious transportation of these massive carved heads is mind-boggling. They would have had to have been dragged – perhaps on a platform rolled over rubber balls. They could have been transported by raft on the river system, but that would have required exceptional raft-making skills to float an object weighing several tons. It would have taken over 1000 men, laboring for months, to get them to their destination.

Archaeological evidence indicates the colossal heads were covered with plaster painted in bright colors. Each head is different, and their faces feature full lips, wide noses, and almond-shaped eyes, some with an epicanthic fold (common in Asians and Polynesians). Some people feel they are African in appearance, or perhaps Asian or Polynesian.

Is this what the Olmec looked like? What were the origins of the Olmec? Some have theorized that the Olmecs were originally from Africa, but DNA studies on two Olmec remains indicate they had DNA consistent with the indigenous populations of the Americas. No specific DNA link has been found between the Olmec and Polynesia or Africa.

Interestingly though, a DNA study published in *Nature* in July 2020 links the ancient Zenú, who lived on the Caribbean side of the country of Columbia, to Easter Island and Fatu Hiva (in Polynesia). Researchers believe this happened around AD 1200, which would have been long after the Olmec civilization, but it does set the imagination racing. Perhaps future archaeological finds and DNA studies will tell us more.

Because the colossal heads can be found at both La Venta and San Lorenzo, we know that producing these massive carvings continued over several centuries. What did they represent? Perhaps each head was that of an Olmec ruler. The heads are carved with some type of head gear, such as a helmet, suggesting an association with the military. Others speculate that the colossal heads represent athletes in the rubber ball games who wore helmets.

The Olmec not only invented rubber balls; they were also known for ball games played by two teams with the rubber ball in a sunken pit. The apparent object of the game was to get the ball to the other end of the court without using their hands (like modern soccer). Depictions in Olmec carvings indicate protective equipment was worn, including helmets. The game was likely an ancient form of the ball game *Ulama*, also played by Aztec and Maya civilizations, and still played today in Mesoamerica. In Ulama, the ball is hit with the hip, upper thigh, or forearm. About 2000 ancient ball courts have been found in Mesoamerica.

Olmec figurine presenting an infant (who appears to be a werejaguar). [vii]

Little is known about the religion and myths of the Olmec, other than what can be gleaned from artifacts. Sacrifice is part of virtually every culture, and it was practiced by the Olmec. Olmec carvings of a person "presenting" an inert baby or small child hints at child sacrifice; partial and complete infant skeletons (found in what are believed to be sacrifice pits) seem to confirm this practice. Other items in the pits suggest sacrifices of metal jewelry, rubber balls, grain, produce, and livestock. Bloodletting, common in later Mesoamerican cultures, is believed to have been part of the sacrificial system, using real and ceramic stingray spikes and shark teeth.

Olmec rulers, priests, and shamans all probably had a part in leading religious activities. They had a jaguar god, along with other supernatural beings that they worshiped. The werejaguar were part of the ancient mythology of the Mesoamericans, including the Olmec. Actual jaguars were at the top of the food chain and had a wide range in ancient times. The werejaguar was probably an Olmec deity representing supremacy and strength. Werejaguar figures had almond eyes, a cleft head, and an open mouth turned downward in a sort of grimace.

Werejaguar sculpture from the Museum of Anthropology at Xalapa, Vera Cruz, Mexico.[viii]

A werejaguar image is sometimes depicted as an infant in the arms of a human man, possibly a shamanic practice of harnessing the fierce power of the jaguar or possibly the mythological offspring of a jaguar mated with a human. Olmec artifacts include jade masks of a jaguar, usually found at shrines, cemeteries, and temples, obviously carrying significant spiritual meaning.

Other deities thought to be worshiped by the Olmec included a dragon or earth monster, depicted in their art as having fangs, eyebrows of fire, and a split tongue. Carvings show a maize deity, with corn growing from his cleft head. The Olmec may have had a rain spirit, and carvings on bowls show what may be some sort of banded-eye god. A feathered serpent, a common deity in many Mesoamerican religions, was found on a stele carving and in a cave painting. Lastly, the Olmec appeared to have had a fish or shark deity.

Recent archeological finds show the Olmec apparently developed an early, very primitive writing system. In the late 1990s, workers building a road in what was the Olmec heartland discovered a block of stone in a pile of bulldozer debris, which also included clay figurines that dated back to the San Lorenzo Olmec period. On the block are 62 glyphs, or elemental symbols, resembling maize, pineapple, fish, and insects, as well as more abstract glyphs. The symbols run horizontally, while other forms of Mesoamerican writing or proto-writing were all vertical, like ancient Chinese writing.

This slab, with its carvings of symbols, generated a lot of controversy. Some scholars hailed it as irrefutable evidence of an early writing system in the Olmec culture. Other scholars felt the slab wasn't as genuinely old as believed or that the symbols weren't a type of writing.

In 1997 and 1998, at an archeological site three miles north of La Venta, three artifacts were uncovered that also appear to point to an Olmec writing system. They dated to about 650 BC, when the

Olmec civilization at La Venta was active. One was a cylinder seal, which, when rolled out, showed a bird "speaking" words (or glyphs). Two fragments of a plaque were found that each contained a glyph similar to glyphs used in later Mesoamerican cultures.

Now, let's move on to what many of us might consider the most interesting aspect of Olmec culture – chocolate! An article in the May 2011 edition of *Proceedings of the National Academy of Sciences* reported on 156 potsherds collected from an archeological dig at San Lorenzo. Residue in the bowls, cups, and bottles was analyzed at the University of California. Testing revealed that 17% of the potsherds had residue containing theobromine, an alkaloid chemical primarily found in the cocoa plant. The Olmec were drinking chocolate! So, the Olmec not only invented rubber balls, but we can also thank them for figuring out how to make chocolate from cacao beans.

As noted earlier, the Olmec culture first emerged in the San Lorenzo area around 1600 BC. In 900 BC, San Lorenzo abruptly declined, and the Olmec city of La Venta rose to prominence as the cultural center or capital city. La Venta developed and dominated until around 400 BC when it also was suddenly evacuated and abandoned. For the next 2000 years, the eastern half of the Olmec heartland was sparsely inhabited. A large segment of the Olmec seemed to have suddenly died out.

La Venta Stela 19, the earliest known representation of the Feathered Serpent in Mesoamerica.[ix]

What caused their eventual extinction? Archeologists believe their depopulation resulted from abrupt and serious changes in the environment to the extent that the area could no longer support a dense population requiring immense agricultural production and a good river system for trade and transport.

We've already speculated on changes to the river courses that likely caused the decline of San Lorenzo. What about La Venta? Tectonic upheaval and shift could have caused earthquakes and volcanic eruptions in the area, as well as further disruption of the river system that the Olmec depended on. Mexico sits on three of the Earth's largest tectonic plates, and earthquakes are common. The soft soil of the marshy Olmec heartland would have amplified the effects of the tremors.

Mexico is the fourth most hazardous country in the world for volcanoes. The San Martin volcano was close to La Venta and erupted as recently as 1796. The El Chichón volcano was also not far away and is still active, last erupting in 1981. The Olmecs lived in the marshy lowlands; even if a volcano isn't erupting, it can leak lethal carbon dioxide, which can collect in low-lying areas, killing humans, animals, and plant life.

The Epi-Olmec

Within a century of the abrupt decline of the Olmec culture, a new culture succeeded it. We refer to them as Epi-Olmec: "epi," meaning "post" or "after." As previously mentioned, the eastern part of the Olmec heartland became a virtual wasteland. However, two cities, Tres Zapotes and Cerro de la Mesas gained prominence in the western part of what was once the Olmec heartland.

The Epi-Olmec culture endured for about 550 years, from 300 BC to AD 250, and seemed to be a gradual transformation from the Olmec culture, rather than a completely new culture gaining dominance. Although not as large and organized as the Olmec, the Epi-Olmecs developed a sophisticated calendar and writing system. However, their trade system did not equal the Olmec, and their art lacked the Olmec refinement.

La Mojarra Stela 1 showing the "Harvester Mountain Lord," AD 156

Several artifacts found in the Epi-Olmec region depict a writing system known as Isthmian script, which may have descended from the Olmec glyphs. In 1986, the *La Mojarra Stela* was unearthed, an extremely important discovery! This carved monument dates to AD 156 and has 535 glyphs. On the right side of the stone is a carving of a man wearing an elaborate headdress with a hook-beaked bird deity and sharks. This – along with his feathered cape – indicate he is a ruler, deity, or priest. Over him are twelve columns of glyphs, and on his right side are eight more columns of glyphs.

In 1997, two linguists, John Justeson and Terrence Kaufman, published a paper saying they had deciphered the script. They reported that the man is the Harvester Mountain Lord and that the writings tell of a solar eclipse and appearances of Venus, how the Mountain Lord came to power, his wars, his own bloodletting, and the sacrifice of his brother-in-law. Some archeologists dispute this translation.

The stone also contained two dates in the form of the Mesoamerican Long Count Calendar, which correspond to the months and years of May AD 143 and July AD 156. The Long Count Calendar was a system that emerged in the Epi-Olmec era and was found in areas influenced by Olmec cultures. It measured time by calculating the number of days from what they considered their creation date, which would have been 3114 BC in our calendar.

Earlier, in 1902, the Tuxtla Statuette was discovered by a farmer in the foothills of the Tuxtlas mountains. The statuette is in the shape of a man with a duck mouth and wings. On it are carved 75 glyphs (known as Isthmian script and corresponding to the La Mojarra Stela) and a Long Count Calendar date which corresponds to AD 162.

The oldest artifact of the Epi-Olmec, containing calendar entries and glyphs, was Stela C. The bottom half of this monument was discovered in 1939 at the Tres Zapotes archeological site (and the location of one of the two leading cities of the Epi-Olmec), and the top half was found in 1969. A Long Count calendar date was carved on this monument that corresponds to September 3, 32 BC. On the back of the stela were carved glyphs in the Epi-Olmec Isthmian script.

We are fortunate to have these glimpses into the Epi-Olmec culture. Everyday life and homes for the common people did not seem to change much in the transition from Olmec to Epi-Olmec. The Epi-Olmec don't seem to have had the centralized hierarchy of the Olmec. By AD 250, their culture gave way to the Classic Veracruz culture, situated a little further north on the Gulf Coast.

Chapter 2: The Toltecs

The Toltec Kingdom, known for legendary sculptors and artists as well as ferocious warrior conquerors, followed the Olmecs as a great Mesoamerican civilization thriving between AD 600 to 1200. The Toltecs were infamous for regularly practicing human sacrifice of adults and children and collecting their skulls on a rack in their ceremonial plaza. They were zealous in spreading the Cult of Quetzalcoatl, the feathered-serpent deity of Mesoamerica and the name their most beloved emperor assumed. The Mexica-Aztecs greatly revered the Toltecs, collected their sculptures and other relics from the Toltec's abandoned city, and claimed to be descended from Toltec royalty.

What were the origins of these warriors and artists? They are believed to have descended from a wild, nomadic people, called the Toltec-Chichimeca, from the deserts of northwestern Mexico and perhaps southern California. In the 9th century, some of these people migrated southward toward the Valley of Mexico: the area encompassing present Mexico City and eastward to the Gulf of Mexico. In their wanderings, the Toltecs picked up cultural influences from the Olmec, the Maya, and, most importantly, the Teotihuacan people.

Pyramid B in Tula.[xi]

According to the oral and pictograph tradition of the Aztecs, some of these nomads settled in Tlachicatzin in the territory of the Hue-Tlapallan people, who called them *Tolteca*, meaning artisan or architect, for their renown as craftsmen and artists. Led by two chiefs, Chalcaltzin and Tlacamihtzin, the Toltecs rebelled against their overlords in AD 544. The Toltecs fought for thirteen years, lost the war, and were exiled.

The exiles traveled to Tlasiculiacan, where they reunited with part of their clan that had fled Tlachicatzin earlier. Together they pressed on, reaching a place called Tlapallanconco, where they lived for three years. But they feared being so close to the Hue-Tlapallan people, so their council of chieftains decided to migrate further.

Their astrologer-priest, Huematzin (the man with the long hand), gave them a prophecy of an uninhabited land in the east where they could live. Hearing this, the Toltecs left part of their clan in Tlapallanconco, and the rest would migrate east. They made a solemn vow they would abstain from sexual relations during the migration, so they could travel without the complications of pregnancies and small children.

They marched east, arriving at Xalisco (Jalisco), where they lived eight years. Leaving some of their people there, they migrated to Chimalhuacan Ateneo. At this point, they decided they'd gone long enough without sex, so they celebrated a conjugal feast, enjoyed relations with their wives, and eventually started having children again. They built boats and settled in the islands of the area, then later lived all together in one large wooden building in a place called Tulantzinco. Finally, in AD 648, after 104 years of nomadic living, they moved to what would be their final home, which they named Tollan (Tula), which literally means *place of the reeds*, indicating abundance.

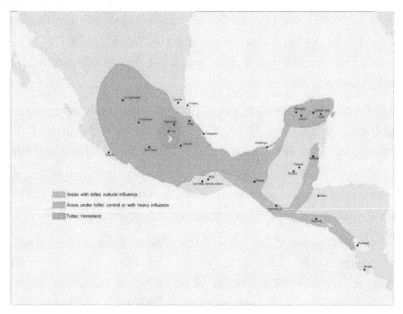

Map of Toltec Influence[xii]

The Toltec core area of Tula was in the region immediately northwest of what is now Mexico City. The extent of Toltec artifacts and architectural influences stretched from the Pacific Ocean to the Gulf of Mexico. Additionally, significant numbers of Toltecs migrated to the Yucatan peninsula in several waves, where they influenced Mayan culture.

Ixtlilcuechahua was one of the earliest Toltec kings, son of Chalchiuhtlanetzin, the chief that founded Tula. Ixtlilcuechahua became king in AD 771, about the age of 37. From his father, he received a legacy of wisdom and good judgment and was loved by his subjects. His greatest task was to establish his once-nomadic people into a civilized society.

Ixtlilcuechahua ruled under the guidance of Huematzin, the priest-prophet who had accompanied the Toltec through their wanderings. The Aztecs said Huematzin chronicled the journeys of the Toltec in the *Teoamoxtli* (Book of the Gods), which also contained the laws, astrology, division of time, sacred rites, and science of the Toltec people. Some scholars question the existence of this book, as no form of writing has been found on Toltec artifacts. Huematzin died at the remarkable age of 300, according to a later Aztec account.

Ixtlilcuechahua made no attempts to conquer peaceful neighboring territories. However, he would fiercely protect Tula from anyone foolish enough to attack the city and then set out to conquer the cities of the attackers, eliminating future threats. This expanded the Toltec territory to include other people and cultures. Ixtlilcuechahua reigned 52 years, apparently resigning in AD 823.

Interestingly, the chronicles of the rulers of Tula show most of them reigned for 52 years, which coincides with the ancient Mesoamerican calendar cycle of 52 years. Some historians question the reliability of the chronicles, concluding they are legendary in nature. However, a mandatory 52-year reign could be a stroke of genius, something like term limits for presidents today. It would help avoid issues like kings with dementia or rulers too feeble to lead their warriors into battle.

The most important Toltec ruler was the priest-king Ce Acatl Topiltzin Quetzalcoatl, believed to have lived from AD 895-947, during the golden age of Tula. One cannot tell the story of the Toltecs without telling the story of Quetzalcoatl. But first, we must mention the Teotihuacan culture flourishing to the east of Tula, which had a strong influence on Toltec culture. Before the Toltecs arrived, the Teotihuacan were worshiping their Lord of Creation, a feathered serpent named Quetzalcoatl.

The story of the man named Quetzalcoatl began when the Toltec king Mixcoatl was out hunting one day and was confronted by a naked woman, Chimalma, whose name meant *hand shield*. For whatever reason, Mixcoatl began shooting arrows at Chimalma, but she was *hand shield*, so she deflected the arrows. This aroused admiration within Mixcoatl, and he fell in love with Chimalma and married her.

After swallowing a precious jade stone, Chimalma became pregnant and gave birth to a son. He was named Ce Acatl Topiltzin, which means *our prince from the year one reed*, because he was born in the first year of the 52-year cycle of the Mesoamerican calendar. Chimalma died in childbirth, and Mixcoatl was assassinated by his own brother, leaving Ce Acatl Topiltzin an orphan. He was raised by his maternal grandparents, who taught him to revere the Teotihuacan god Quetzalcoatl. The prince eventually took on the name Quetzalcoatl out of admiration for the feathered serpent.

After avenging his father's death, Ce Acatl Topiltzin Quetzalcoatl became Emperor of the Toltecs, bringing in new knowledge, including advanced agricultural methods for corn and cacao beans (chocolate). Topiltzin Quetzalcoatl ruled over an orderly and harmonious city of wealth and brilliant artistry. During Quetzalcoatl's reign, the city of Tula built a new district for the major religious and political buildings, known today as *Tula Grande* (Great Tula).

Ce Acatl Topiltzin Quetzalcoatl.

Fragment of a mural by Diego Rivera in the Palacio Nacional (Mexico City)[viii]

Seeking to transform Toltec society, Quetzalcoatl outlawed human sacrifice. Beloved by his people as a peaceful, merciful, and just priest-ruler, he never sacrificed humans, but only birds, snakes, and butterflies. Migrants from several ethnic groups began flooding the city, perhaps drawn by the wise and benevolent ruler Quetzalcoatl.

Quetzalcoatl's idyllic reign ended when Tezcatlipoca, the *smoke and mirrors god,* tricked him with a mirror which made Quetzalcoatl look deformed. Tezcatlipoca then handed Quetzalcoatl a drink: "Just swallow this, and you will look young and handsome again!" Quetzalcoatl invited his sister to drink the "medicine" with him. Unknown to them, the drink held hallucinogens, and they ended up behaving disgracefully. The next morning, they were found naked, lying next to each other.

Ashamed and humiliated, Quetzalcoatl abdicated his priesthood and crown. For the next year, he wandered from village to village, trying to purge his sin by continuous bloodletting. Finally, he arrived at the Gulf of Mexico, built a funeral pyre, and set himself on fire. Legend says thousands of quetzal birds flew out of the fire. After his death, he descended into the underworld, where he outwitted Mictlantecuhtli, god of the dead, and then ascended into the heavens to become Venus, the morning star.

In a different and more popular version of the story, Quetzalcoatl sailed out to sea on a raft of serpents, vowing that one day he would return in the *year of one reed*. This refers to the 52-year calendar cycle, which had a reed for each year. He was born in the year of one reed, left the earth 52 years later in a year of one reed, and would come back in another year of one reed. Quetzalcoatl promised he would return to the same spot from which he was leaving to overthrow Tezcatlipoca and restore his utopian kingdom. Legends say that just as his raft reached the horizon, it exploded, and Quetzalcoatl shot up into the sky to become Venus.

According to some historians, this alternative version played a pivotal role when, in AD 1519, the Spanish conquistador Cortés sailed in from the Gulf of Mexico. This was *a year of one reed* in the Aztec calendar. The Aztec king Moctezuma apparently believed Cortés was Quetzalcoatl returning to claim his kingdom, according to some. However, as we will learn later, Moctezuma didn't exactly welcome Cortés with open arms.

At any rate, once Quetzalcoatl was out of the way, the trickster Tezcatlipoca usurped the city of Tula, demanding human sacrifice. The golden age was no more, and a pronounced decline of the Toltec empire ensued. Thousands of Toltecs left Tula around AD

981, mostly heading to the Yucatan Peninsula and the city of Uxmal.

The myth likely has a basis in fact. When the Toltecs first arrived at Tula, they favored a peaceful theocracy led by a righteous priest-king. The legend of Quetzalcoatl being outwitted by Tezcatlipoca probably represents an actual military coup that overturned the theocracy and set up a more violent military dictatorship, as the Toltecs eventually became infamous for brutal conquest and human sacrifice.

Another intriguing royal Toltec was Empress Xochitl, who rose from peasant to power. Her father, Papantzin, invented *pulque*, a favorite Mesoamerican drink made from the fermented syrup of the maguey (agave) plant. His daughter Xochitl carried a bowl of pulque as a gift to Emperor Tecpancaltzin, who was enchanted with Xochitl and enjoyed the unusual beverage.

Xochitl with father Papantzin offering pulque to Emperor.
(Obregón, 1869) [xiv]

Xochitl would occasionally bring the emperor more bowls of pulque, and her charm won him over. He elevated Papantzin to land-holding nobility, and Xochitl became his concubine. Xochitl gave birth to a son named Meconetzin, meaning *child of maguey*, who became crown prince, as Tecpancaltzin's first wife, Maxio, had only daughters. After Maxio died, Xochitl became Empress.

During Tecpancaltzin's reign, an ethnic-religious civil war erupted between the mostly Nonoalca worshipers of Quetzalcoatl and the Chichimeca, who worshiped his archrival Tezcatlipoca. The conflict centered on human sacrifice, which Quetzalcoatl had forbidden, but which Tezcatlipoca's followers believed was intrinsic to keeping the gods happy.

When the war broke out, Xochitl called her fellow women out to battle, leading an entirely female battalion. Both Xochitl and her husband died on the battlefield, and the battle was lost. Most followers of the Cult of Quetzalcoatl fled to the Yucatan, where they were welcomed by their clansmen, descendants of those who had previously emigrated from Tula after Quetzalcoatl had abdicated.

Chac Mool[v]

The Toltecs were well-known for their beautiful carvings and artwork. One intriguing example, distinctive to Toltec culture, are *Chac Mool* stone figurines reclining back on their elbows and holding a bowl on their chests. The Toltecs made exquisite gold and turquoise jewelry such as nose rings, elegant masks of jade, and carved human and jaguar standard-bearers. They created fine metalwork and stunning architectural features such as serpent columns and massive porticoes.

Along with their artistry, the Toltecs were noted for warfare. In the latter part of their civilization, warfare was essentially a religion, and the warrior class was viewed with honor and distinction. Warriors were highly trained, fierce, and formidable. The higher ranks of the thoroughly organized and efficient Toltec military wore padded cotton armor to deflect spears and arrows. The soldiers carried round shields and swords into battle. Their helmets were decorated with quetzal plumes, they wore nose rings as a sign of their nobility, and some had beards.

Quetzalcoatl the Feathered Serpent[xvi]

The Toltecs had several major deities. Quetzalcoatl, worshiped by many other Mesoamerican people, was considered the wisest of all beings, creator of the universe, and god of wind, air, and learning. In Toltec art, Quetzalcoatl was depicted as the feathered serpent or as a man with a beard. Quetzalcoatl's beard is somewhat curious, as bearded men were uncommon among the indigenous Mesoamericans. Perhaps the Toltecs had more facial hair, as carvings and paintings of Toltec warriors also show some with beards.

Tlaloc was the cloud deity, both the benevolent giver of rain and the destructive god of storms. He was married to Xochiquetzal, the goddess of beauty, love, and youth. She could be erratic, doing things like seducing a priest, then turning him into a scorpion.

Tezcatlipoca, Quetzalcoatl's nemesis but sometimes considered to be his brother, had the nickname *Smoking Mirror* due to tricking Quetzalcoatl with the magic mirror. He was the god of the night, of time, and of memory. He was also a creator God.

Centeotl was Lord of the Maize, the predominant crop in Mesoamerica. Corn, or maize, was gifted to humans by Quetzalcoatl, but Centeotl was the maintainer of the crop's growth and fertility. He held the key to successful agriculture, which he taught to humans.

The ceremonial plaza at Tula contained temples and pyramids where Toltec deities were worshiped, ballgames played, and people sacrificed. The partially excavated Pyramid C, the Temple of the Sun, is probably a temple of Quetzalcoatl. Pyramid B is the temple of Tlahuizcalpantecuhtli, or Venus, an incarnation of Quetzalcoatl.

Atlantes of Pyramid B at Tula[xvii]

Astonishing columns, carved to represent warriors, are called the *Atlantes of Tula*, the most dominant architecture associated with the Toltecs. Just as the Olmecs are known for their colossal heads, the Toltecs are defined by the Atlantean columns. They are called Atlanteans (or Atlantes) because they carry at their side the *atlatl*, a spear-throwing tool that leverages a spear's velocity. The Atlanteans are close to 15 feet high and held up the roofs of the great rooms of the temples.

The Toltec Temple B was decorated with carvings, depicting a row of jaguars, under which were carvings of Venus, followed by a row of coyotes, followed by a row of eagles, each devouring a heart. These symbols represented the ranks of the military. Next to the Temple of Venus are pillared hallways for festive occasions.

In the temple complex of Tula are two ball courts. The Toltecs loved ball games as much as the Olmecs. On the side of one ball court is a sweat lodge, where players would purify themselves before and after the games. Benches are found throughout the temple complex with carved images of the Feathered Serpent over a procession of warriors. In the middle of the temple complex is a small altar, with a skull rack next to it, another Toltec distinctive.

Chichén Itzá Pyramid[xviii]

The influence of Toltec migrants in the Yucatan area is clearly seen in the ruins of Chichén Itzá. Archeology suggests that the Itzá people were either Toltec or strongly influenced by the Toltec people. The pyramid in Chichén Itzá is a temple to Quetzalcoatl (Kukulkan) that showcases the Toltec influence. The Temple of the Warriors in Chichén Itzá mirrors Temple B in Tula, with all its colonnades and a Chac Mool figurine in front of two images of Quetzalcoatl. The largest ballcourt in Mesoamerica is found in the temple complex of Chichén Itzá, with the Toltec skull rack just next to it.

The Toltec capital city of Tula (Tollan) was one of the largest cities in pre-Columbian Mesoamerica, with an estimated population of 85,000. Large apartment complexes housed most of the urban population, with the ruling elite living in palaces. Distinct sections separated citizens of different classes. Most structures were of stone covered with adobe mud.

Tula society was ruled by an aristocracy of warriors and priests. The cherished artisans, who gave the Toltecs their name, formed the middle class, along with merchants. Tula was dependent on agriculture to feed the large population, so farmers were given special rights and privileges. The many immigrants likely served in the working class. Accounts speak of Toltec warriors carrying the weeping Huastec people and others into Tula; the captives were likely facing slavery, or worse yet, human sacrifice.

What caused the artistic yet warlike Toltec civilization to be assimilated by other kingdoms and fade away? One element was the ongoing internal conflict between the two dominant ethnic groups: the Nonoalca worshipers of Quetzalcoatl and the Chichimeca worshipers of Tezcatlipoca. A seven-year drought, from AD 1070 to 1077, caused a collapse in the agricultural system, and the population was decimated by starvation. Many survivors migrated to more fertile areas.

Tula was invaded by the Chichimeca people from the north in AD 1115. War raged for a year, each side sacrificing their prisoners-of-war to their deities, ending with the Toltec defeat. Huemac, king of Tula, fled with his citizens, creating a Toltec diaspora across Mexico. Most of Tula was abandoned, with the Toltec remnant ruled by surrounding city-states.

The *Codex Boturini*, an ancient Aztec manuscript written soon after the Spaniards arrived, depicts the early migration of the Aztec-Mexica people through Tula, where they stopped for twenty years. This would have been about AD 1250, and by this time, most Toltecs had abandoned Tula. The Mexica spent twenty years among the remnant of the population, surrounded by the Toltec architecture and artifacts, soaking in the Toltec culture they so deeply admired.

Desiring to claim descendancy from the Toltecs, the Mexica married their princesses to the remaining Toltec nobility. The Mexica not only absorbed Toltec culture during their stay in Tula, but they also appropriated many Toltec relics, which later showed up in their own cities.

Chapter 3: The Chichimeca

Children of the Wind was what they called themselves; when running or climbing, it appeared these people were carried by the wind. Other cultures called them *Chichimeca*, carrying the idea of *barbarian*. That's how these roaming tribes were regarded by other civilizations of Mesoamerica: the ones who had built cities with majestic temples and palaces and developed advanced agriculture and written languages. And yet, the untamed Chichimeca remained undefeated by the Spanish invaders, to whom more civilized cultures swiftly fell. Several Chichimeca tribal groups still exist today, speaking their ancient languages and maintaining elements of their primeval cultures.

Chichimeca is an umbrella term for multiple groups of nomadic and semi-nomadic people belonging to the larger Nahuatl language group who originally lived in the deserts of northern Mexico. Although usually painted with a broad brush, they were individual cultures of around seven to ten tribes. They shared the same language group, but they spoke distinct dialects, often unintelligible from one another. We might think of the Nahuatl language group as something like the Romance language group, with the differences between Spanish, Italian, French, Romanian, and Portuguese. The main similarities shared by the Chichimeca tribes were the harsh living conditions of the lands they inhabited and their nomadic lifestyle.

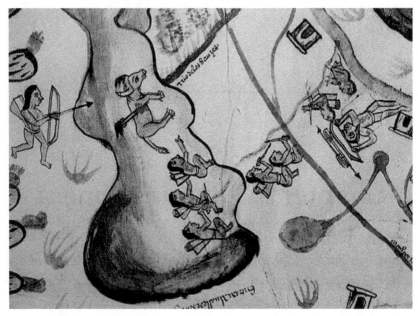

Images from a 1580 map of San Miguel and San Felipe in the Chichimeca region, Juan Carlos Fonseca Mata.[xix]

Most of what we know about the Chichimeca tribes is what other civilizations recorded about them, such as the Aztecs and eventually the Spaniards. The Chichimeca had no written language of their own, and they didn't build temples or other permanent structures that could later be studied by archaeologists. Their lifestyle was so simple that they left almost no historical imprint, other than observations by others and what is left of their culture in the remnant Chichimeca tribes of today.

The great Toltec civilization had its origins in one Chichimeca tribe, the Tolteca-Chichimeca, which drifted south and eventually settled down and built a great city. More waves of Chichimeca migrations infiltrated their ranks until the Toltecs struggled in an internal war between the earlier and later cultures. Eventually, attacked by another Chichimeca tribe, the Toltecs lost the war and fled their great city. Thus, it could be said that the Chichimeca gave birth to the Toltecs and later served as their executioners.

The Mexica-Aztecs were probably another Chichimeca tribe. While the Olmecs and Toltecs were building great temples and pyramids, the Mexica were subsisting in the northern wilderness. Finally, they migrated south, learned from the Toltec and other civilizations, developed their own written language and astounding Aztec culture, and became the chroniclers of previous cultures as well as their own Chichimeca origins.

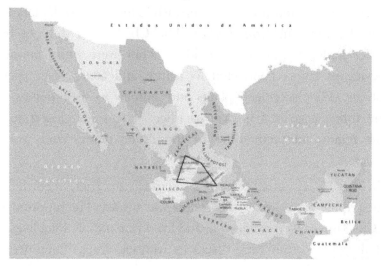

Bajio region of Mexico[xx]

As hunters and gatherers, the Chichimeca roamed the harsh deserts of northern Mexico that extended into Arizona and California until some of the tribes migrated in several waves into the rugged mountains and arid areas of central Mexico. A sizeable population of Chichimeca established themselves in the lowland Bajio region of central Mexico, in today's states of Aguascalientes, Jalisco, Guanajuato, and Querétaro. Their region encompassed about 62,000 square miles. In the days before the Spanish invasion, few permanent settlements existed in this area.

Before the arrival of the Spaniards, most tribes were nomadic or semi-nomadic desert dwellers. They hunted game and gathered cacti fruit, agave plants, berries, roots, and mesquite beans for food. The tribes who lived in the southernmost area of the broad Chichimeca heartland, closest to the Aztec civilization, engaged in primitive farming, mostly raising squash and maize.

They went mostly naked, covering only their genitals with animal skins or cloth woven from the maguey plant. As many as 60,000 Chichimeca roamed the plains of central and northern Mexico, living in caves or temporary shelters, while the more sedentary lived in small settlements (*rancherias*). The Chichimeca did not build temples and generally had no idols. They were more animistic, believing in spirits connected to nature and attached to specific locations. They sacrificed plants and animals to their deities, and some tribes practiced human sacrifice. The ones closest to the Aztec region adopted some of the Aztec deities and worship practices.

In the 16th century, Sahagún, a Franciscan friar, recorded his ethnographic research in the *Florentine Codex*. He reported that the Chichimeca were seldom ill and lived remarkably long lives. He said they could run long distances without tiring. Their women would give birth and then rejoin the group's activity without pausing to rest.

Four of the Chichimeca nations, with decentralized governments and overlapping territories, became a great irritant to the Spanish conquistadors. These tribes – the Guachichiles, the Pames, the Guamares, and the Zacatecos – formed a loose alliance to successfully defeat the Spaniards' attempts to subjugate them and colonize their lands. Although there were several other Chichimeca tribes, we know more about these four from Spanish accounts.

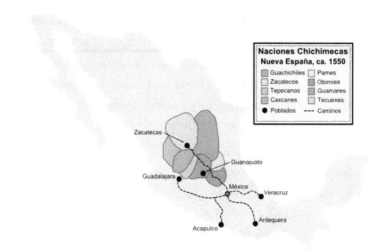

Territory of Chichimeca Nations[xxi]

What is now the city of San Luis Potosí is roughly at the center of the large area around which the Guachichiles tribal group roamed. The largest of the four groups, they assumed leadership of the Chichimeca Confederation. Their name comes from their fondness for the color red; they dyed their hair, skin, and clothing red. They delighted in collecting scalps of Spanish men with red hair, and they enjoyed kidnapping or purchasing red-haired European women to be their wives. Even today, a red-haired child is occasionally born to their descendants.

The Guachichiles were fierce fighters and expert hunters, extremely skilled in archery. Children learned to use a bow when they began walking. The velocity, strength, and sharpness of their arrows were incredible, able to penetrate the Spaniards' metal armor. They could easily survive in the cacti-filled terrain they called home, knowing where to find food and water. They battled their rivals with cunning and subterfuge rather than direct attacks. They employed spies to assess their adversaries' strengths and weaknesses and to follow their movements. They would ambush their enemies, striking fear by suddenly jumping out wearing animal heads and red paint and howling and shrieking – they even scared the horses!

The Pame people were more docile than the neighboring Guachichiles and more likely to assimilate the religion and culture of the developed civilizations. They were traders, so it was to their advantage to get along with everybody and learn the dialects of those around them. Their adaptability aided their survival into our modern world as a Chichimeca tribe whose culture endures today.

The Pames were enigmatic, outwardly complying with the Spanish requirement to live clustered around missions and submit to Catholic indoctrination while quietly worshiping their own deities, following the guidance of their shamans, and practicing their traditional dances. Even today, the 10,000 Pame-language-speaking people living in Santa Maria Acapulco are syncretistic: nominal Catholics who continue to practice their traditional religion.

The Guamare tribe called themselves *Children of the Wind* for their tradition of cremating their dead and throwing their ashes into the wind. Living in the mountains of what today is Guanajuato state, they were shrewd, fearless, and known for double-crossing others. Like the Guachichiles, they enjoyed coloring their hair and bodies – sometimes red, sometimes white, and sometimes other colors, depending on their clan. They tattooed their bodies, and both men and women wore their hair down to their waists.

The fourth tribe in the Chichimeca Confederation were the Zacatecos, living in what is now the states of Durango and Zacatecas, where they overlapped with the Guachichiles. Descendants of this tribe still live in the area, but they have largely abandoned their culture and traditions. In days of old, some were nomads, while others cultivated maize. They wore animal-skin shin-guards to protect themselves from the thorny bushes and cacti, and they sometimes wore leather sandals.

Member of Chichimeca Jonaz tribe

Juan Bautista de Pomar, a 16th-century mestizo historian, wrote that the Zacatecos were "graceful, strong, robust, and beardless" and "the best archers in the world." The Zacatecos deities were celestial: the sun, moon, and several stars. They did not practice human sacrifice but worshiped with flowers, herbs, and dancing.

When the Spaniards arrived in Mexico, far to the south of the Chichimeca lands, their initial concern was conquering the Aztecs, which they did two years later. Most of the other civilizations in Mexico quickly submitted to Spanish rule or were conquered after a few battles. The Spaniards' main interest was collecting and mining gold and other precious minerals and establishing colonies in fertile areas.

The Chichimeca were of scant interest to the Spaniards initially, as their lands were generally unsuitable for farming, and they had nothing the Spaniards considered valuable. In a 1526 letter, Hernán Cortés wrote that the uncivilized Chichimeca might be useful as slave labor in the mines. The Spaniards apparently did not tap this potential labor source; if they tried, the Chichimeca probably proved too difficult to tame.

Then, in AD 1546, the Spaniards learned that silver-rich ore existed close to the Zacatecas territory. Excited by this discovery and eager for quick wealth, hundreds of Spaniards migrated north to the Chichimeca heartland, which they called *La Gran Chichimeca.* They began digging silver mines, building roads, and establishing towns. The Chichimeca tribes resented this intrusion on their sacred, ancestral lands and retaliated with guerilla warfare, attacking caravans of goods moving through their territory.

The conflict in the Bajio region became the forty-year Chichimeca War (1550-1590), the lengthiest and most costly military campaign in the history of the Spanish Empire in Mesoamerica. The Chichimeca raided and pillaged Spanish settlements and caravans, and the Spaniards attempted to vanquish them with a strategy of *fire and blood*, but the Chichimeca proved undefeatable.

Portrait of Chichimeca Jonaz dancers at Ceremonial Center, Mision Chichimecas; live direct descendants of Chichimeca[xxii]

Primarily nomads, the Chichimeca had few settlements for the Spaniards to target, and they were adapted to the rough terrain. They knew how to live off the land, but the Spanish invaders depended on livestock, agriculture, and imported supplies. By ambushing the Spanish caravans and raiding their settlements, the Chichimeca effectively cut off the Spaniards' food and weapons supply while enriching themselves with the Spanish livestock and goods. The four tribes in the Chichimeca Confederation had joined forces to fight the Spaniards, but even the more distant tribes came to raid the Spaniards, lured by the loot.

The Chichimeca legendary archery skills were a force to reckon with. Their lethal arrowheads of volcanic obsidian, sharper than razors, penetrated the chain-mail armor of the Spaniards. Even when outnumbered four to one, the Chichimeca defeated the Spaniards in battle. Before attacking a Spanish town, they would first send in spies to gather strategic details and then steal their horses to slow down the Spaniards. At first, the Chichimeca ate the horses they stole but quickly learned to ride them, which made them swift in their ongoing raids on the Spaniards.

In desperation, the Spaniards began building forts, hiring mercenaries, and training their indigenous slaves to fight. Eleven years into the war, the Chichimeca had killed over 4000 Spaniards and their Mesoamerican allies. The Spanish policy of *fire and blood* threatened to kill, enslave, or mutilate every Chichimeca warrior. Yet the Chichimeca dominated the struggle. The Chichimeca Confederation used their combined numbers and diverse skills to cut off roads, raid towns, and damage mines.

Spain dug into the royal treasury to fund military forces, weapons, and materials for forts, but the Chichimeca continued attacking with even greater ferocity, essentially shutting down the silver mines and destroying the royal roads and all the Spanish forts within the Guachichiles territory. The Spaniards were no match for the Chichimeca Confederation. The war of fire and blood was a failure, and the Spanish royal treasury was decimated. The Spaniards were confounded; they had conquered the Aztecs with only 500 or 600 men but could not conquer the Chichimeca even with thousands of soldiers.

Artwork from 1580 map of Chichimeca areas of San Miguel and San Felipe, Juan Carlos Fonseca Mata[xxiii]

Some Spanish clerics had become appalled by Spanish mistreatment of Chichimeca women and children and by the killings or mutilations of their captive warriors. The clergy pointed out that Spanish callousness and cruelty had stirred up the initial conflict and was perpetuating the antipathy of the Chichimeca. The Dominicans declared in 1574 that the war against the Chichimeca was unjust and that continued aggression would only further inflame the Chichimeca's hostility and prolong the conflict. Could there be a different, more gentle way to bring peace with the Chichimeca while still permitting the Spaniards to mine the land?

The Bishop of Guadalajara came up with a proposal in 1584, which he called a "Christian remedy." Instead of conquering or killing the Chichimeca, his plan was to Christianize them. He suggested establishing peaceful villages throughout the Chichimeca heartland, inhabited by indigenous people who would be friendly with the Chichimeca and by priests who could teach the Catholic faith. To end the conflict, the bishop recommended that the Spaniards change their policy to purchasing peace and gently assimilating the Chichimeca into Spanish culture.

In 1585, Álvaro Manrique de Zúñiga became Viceroy of *New Spain* (the Spanish colonies in the Americas and the Pacific islands). He liked the bishop's proposal and decided to implement it. His first step was to remove most of the Spanish military from the Chichimeca area. They weren't proving effective against the Chichimeca, and he felt their presence was an affront to the indigenous people, provoking violence rather than stemming it. Manrique de Zúñiga then began negotiations with the Chichimeca leaders. He promised an end to Spanish military operations and offered land, food, farm animals, clothing, and tools in exchange for peace.

Captain Miguel Caldera, who was part-Chichimeca, of Spanish and Guachichiles descent, was a key negotiator in implementing the *Purchase for Peace* program. He negotiated peace treaties between the Spaniards and the tribal groups. Large quantities of food, clothing, goods, plows, hoes, and livestock were sent north to the Chichimeca to persuade them to end the raids. They were also promised freedom from taxes and forced service.

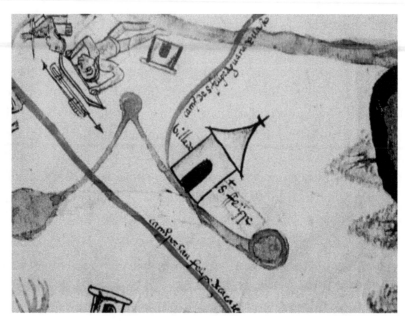

Late 1500's map showing settlements around a mission church.
Juan Carlos Fonseca Mata.[xxiv]

The next step was to move 400 families of the indigenous Tlaxcala people into the area to establish eight settlements. The Tlaxcala were old allies of the Spaniards from the south, who had helped them bring down the Aztecs. The plan was for the Tlaxcala to befriend the Chichimeca, teach them how to raise crops and livestock, serve as Christian examples, and gently persuade the Chichimeca tribes to settle in villages. The Tlaxcala people agreed to move into the area in exchange for land grants, tax freedom, two years of food, and the right to bear arms.

Another important step was to end the slave-raids of the Chichimeca people by arresting the guilty parties (including Spanish soldiers). As the Chichimeca gradually settled into villages, Franciscan and Jesuit missionary-priests who had learned the tribal dialects were sent to the settlements to convert the Chichimeca to Christianity. Over time, more Chichimeca abandoned their nomadic lifestyle to become farmers and ranchers. Gradually, the Chichimeca were integrated into "civilized" society and adopted nominal Catholicism. By 1590, the roads in the Zacatecas region were finally safe; after forty years of warfare, peace had come.

When military conquest had failed, the new Spanish policy of peace with the Chichimeca was based on four pillars: 1) negotiating peace treaties by providing food and other goods and removing soldiers and slave-traders that were provoking the Chichimeca; 2) encouraging conversion to the Catholic faith; 3) moving indigenous allies to the Bajio region to serve as examples and teachers, and 4) providing the means (including livestock and tools) for the Chichimeca to settle into villages. The new policy succeeded in ending the war, and the Spaniards continued to use this strategy on other frontiers of New Spain.

The new Spanish policy of Purchase for Peace worked well for the Spanish; they reopened the silver mines, safely travel on the roads in Le Grande Chichimeca, and no longer feared the tribal people. Fourteen monasteries were scattered through the area. However, for most of the Chichimeca, it was the end of their culture. They no longer roamed free and wild, living off what the land offered them.

Now, they were working the fields and mines, along with the Aztecs, Tlaxcala, and other indigenous people with more developed cultures. The Chichimeca began to absorb this Mestizo culture, with a blend of Spanish and indigenous traditions, as their own way of life faded away. Most tribes lost their languages, their lifestyle, and their traditions until they each became virtually extinct as a culture. A few groups struggled on into modern society, but they have been forced into small reservations on inhospitable land, making survival difficult. The mighty and untamed children of the wind were bribed into abandoning their identity.

PART TWO

THE RISE OF THE AZTEC CIVILIZATION

Chapter 4: Aztec Origins and Mythical Aztlan

About 850 years ago, a nomadic people wandered into the highlands plateau of the Valley of Mexico. Great civilizations had risen and fallen in this area for over a thousand years: Cuicuilco, buried under the lava of the Xitle volcano, Teotihuacan, and the Toltec Empire. Now the stately pyramids, majestic temples, and impressive carvings of past civilizations were largely abandoned, but new settlements were rapidly springing up.

The newcomers were the Nahuatl-speaking Mexica, also called Aztec, after their mysterious home country of Aztlan they had left over 100 years earlier. Who were these people, and where did they come from? How did they define themselves? Was their ancestral home of Aztlan mythical or a real place?

Based on their language group (Nahuatl) and their descriptions of their wanderings through the northern area full of cacti spines, thistles, and poisonous lizards, the Mexica were likely a branch of the Chichimeca tribes, subsisting in the desert before they settled in the Valley of Mexico. The Mexica-Aztecs themselves presented their origins as Chichimeca but also Toltec.

The hunter-warrior aspect of the Chichimeca likely resonated with them. The Chichimeca represented virality, strength, skill in battle, the ability to thrive in harsh conditions, cunning, and fearlessness – all characteristics of the perfect warrior the Aztecs strove to become.

The Mexica-Aztecs also admired the once-nomadic Toltecs, who rose from their own Tolteca-Chichimeca origins to develop a great civilization. They were role models for the Mexica, who aspired to emulate their rise to power and take it to a higher plane. The Mexica-Aztecs prided themselves on being an evolving people, always advancing, always rising to the next level.

The Aztecs defined themselves as descendants of fierce nomads who had risen to fulfill their destiny as warriors, conquerors, and empire builders. They considered their history as an extended military campaign of making war on provinces and cities and subjugating them. The Mexica-Aztec claimed they were following the prophecy of their chief god, Huitzilopochtli, the enemy of tranquility and friend of contention. They considered the concepts of peace and maintaining the status quo as impediments to achieving what was foreordained.

And yet, there was a time when they weren't nomads or empire builders. There was a time when, according to their legends, they once lived a peaceful life as agriculturalists and fishermen in their idyllic island of Aztlan. What can we know about this mysterious land and its location?

Page 3 of Codex Boturini showing the journey of Aztecs from Aztlan to the Valley of Mexico[xxv]

We can glean some understanding about the origins of these people from several Aztec manuscripts written in the 16th century, either just before or after the Spanish conquistadors arrived. They include the *Codex Boturini,* the *Crónica Mexicáyotl,* the *Codex Ramirez,* the *Codex Aubin,* and *Los Anales de Tlatelolco.* We also have histories written by early Spanish chroniclers, based on their study of Aztec documents and interviews with the Aztec people. These include *Monarquía Indiana (Indian Monarchy),* written in 1615 by Friar Juan de Torquemada, and *Historia de las Indias de Nueva España (History of the Indians of New Spain)* by Friar Diego Durán (ca.1537-1588).

The Mexica-Aztecs said they came from an idyllic place called Aztlan. Where was Aztlan? Can we find any linguistic clues from the meaning of the name? In the Nahuatl language, the suffix *lan* or *tlan* means *the place of,* and the suffix *tec* means *people from.* So, *Aztec* means *people from Az* or *Azt,* and *Aztlan* means *place of Az* or *Azt.* What does the prefix *Az* or *Azt* mean? Linguists and historical documents have presented several options.

The Aztec chronicle *Crónica Mexicáyotl* says Aztlan means *place of herons.* The Nahuatl word *aztatl* means *heron or egret,* putting together the Nahuatl prefix *azt,* which frequently refers to a heron or heron plumage or a bird, with the suffix *atl* for *water.* This would fit with the description of Aztlan as an island on a lake filled with waterfowl.

Some linguists say that Aztlan means *white place* because the Nahuatl word *aztapiltic* means something very white. However, this word for white takes us back to the idea of *heron;* it basically means *heron color* by combining the prefix for heron with the suffix *iltic* that carries the idea of color. Many Nahuatl words for colors end with *ic, itc, ltic,* or *iltic.*

A third idea is that Aztlan means *place of tools.* The rationale for this meaning is that in the Nahuatl language, *āz* (or *huaztli*) is a *morpheme* (word part) that changes a noun into a different noun that could be used to produce something. For instance, the word *log* in Nahuatl is *tepontli,* but inserting *āz* into the word changes it to *teponāztli,* meaning *drum.* Linguistically, this is a bit of a stretch because one must have a noun to insert *āz* into for this to work. With *Aztlan,* we don't have a noun – just the suffix *tlan* or *lan,* meaning *place of.*

In summary, the strongest definition for Aztlan from a linguistic standpoint is *place of (white) herons.* This is what the Aztecs themselves said it meant in the *Crónica Mexicáyotl,* and it also fits with the description of the island paradise that would have herons along the shore. Furthermore, herons and heron plumage played an important part in Aztec culture – they formed elaborate headdresses from the plumes of this bird and decorated their ceremonial areas and sacred objects with heron feathers.

According to their history, the Mexica left their home of Aztlan around AD 1168 and wandered almost two centuries before reaching the island on the swampy lake where they would build their city. They were led by their chieftain Tenoch, the son of Iztac

Mixcoatl. Mixcoatl had two wives and seven sons and may have been a real person, but in both Toltec and Aztec mythology, he is identified as the god of the hunt. You might remember him in the earlier chapter on the Toltecs as the hunter and king who married Chimalma and became father to Ce Acatl Topiltzin, who later called himself Quetzalcoatl.

Tenoch, Mexica chieftain, from the Codex Mendoza[xxvi]

Even though of royal birth as the son of Mixcoatl, Tenoch was elected chieftain by a council of elders and was held in great respect by the people he led on their great southern migration. Throughout their history, the Mexica nobility and priests elected their leaders. When the Mexica finally reached their ultimate destination at Lake Texcoco, they named their island settlement Tenochtitlan in honor of this esteemed chieftain. Another name for the Mexica was Tenochca, people of the great chieftain who guided them to the place where they would soon build an empire.

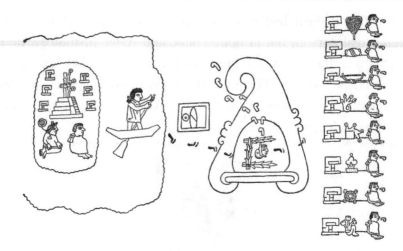

Leaving Aztlan, from the Codex Boturini.[xxvii]

The first page of the *Codex Boturini* has a picture of the island of Aztlan with a pyramid. The picture indicates that a priest led the Mexica and their ancestress Chimalma from Aztlan on a boat. Interestingly, the Mexica-Aztecs claimed both Mixcoatl and Chimalma as their ancestors. These two were the parents of Emperor Ce Acatl Topiltzin Quetzalcoatl in Toltec history. Were the Mexica trying to claim legitimacy by adopting this couple as their own ancestors? Or were they really from the same clan and just migrated several centuries later?

The rest of the *Codex Boturini* chronicles the migration of the Mexica and their history from AD 1168 to 1355. It doesn't give much information about Aztlan itself, except that it mentions that after the Mexica left Aztlan, their god Huitzilopochtli taught them how to sacrifice blood and that they first offered human sacrifice. From that, we can infer that human sacrifice and blood sacrifice were not a part of the Aztlan culture.

An interesting trend in Mesoamerica was building cities on an island in a lake or swampy area. Ancient sources say Aztlan was an island in a lake called *Metztliapan* or *Lake of the Moon,* with a great hill called *Colhuacan* (or *Coatepec).* The people of the island were said to enjoy all they needed to live. The waters around Aztlan were filled with waterfowl, including herons and ducks. The people caught beautiful large fish from their canoes and tended floating *Chinampas* gardens of peppers, tomatoes, and maize. Exquisite red and yellow birds fluttered in the shade trees that lined the banks of the island, filling the air with song.

Seven tribes emerging from seven caves[xxviii]

In the hill called Colhuacan on the island (or near the island) were located seven caves from which seven tribes emerged: the Xochimilca, Tlahuica, Acolhua, Tlaxcalteca, Tepaneca, Chalca, and Mexica. Each tribe left, one by one, to migrate and settle in different areas. The Mexica were the last tribe to leave. Perhaps these seven tribes were the seven sons of Iztac Mixcoatl, father of the Mexica chieftain Tenoch. Since they all came from Aztlan, all seven tribes can be collectively called Aztec.

Where was Aztlan located? The answer is shrouded in mystery. One clue, from tracing their linguistic lineage, is that the Aztec tribes were from the lands north of Mexico City. The Aztecs spoke the Nahuatl language, which has given us words in English, including coyote, tomato, chocolate, avocado, and chili. Nahuatl is from the Uto-Aztecan language family, which extends from Mexico to the southwestern United States, leading to speculation that the Aztecs may have come from north of the border.

Their description of floating gardens in the waters surrounding Aztlan is fascinating. Did the Aztecs carry this custom with them? The Xochimilca, another Nahuatl-speaking culture said to be among the seven tribes from Aztlan, were well-known for *chinampas* or floating gardens constructed from reed rafts covered with mud from the lake. On these rafts, the people grew vegetables, fruit, and flowers, which they shipped two miles to the Aztec capital Tenochtitlan. The research of anthropologist and archaeologist Richard Blanton dates the chinampa settlements on Lake Xochimilco to AD 1100, meaning they were there before the Mexica arrived, but the Xochimilca were another Aztec tribe who may have imported the technology from Aztlan.

A confusing aspect of the Aztec origins is what or who *Chicomoztoca* was. Some accounts say Chicomoztoca was the cave from which the seven tribes were birthed. Others say the Chicomoztoca were a people who preceded the seven tribes and were less civilized. The *Codex Aubin* says the Aztecs left Aztlan because of the tyranny of a ruling elite called Azteca Chicomoztoca. Other accounts mention Chicomoztoca as being a place near Aztlan, but not on Aztlan itself. Were the Mexica of Aztlan perhaps vassals of a nearby nation? Had they been conquered by a people called Chicomoztoca? Or was it a place of refuge after leaving Aztlan?

Why did the Mexica and other Aztec tribes leave their idyllic Aztlan? Perhaps some internal struggle or attack from another tribe or overlord forced them to leave their blissful island. They could have also been affected by some natural disaster, such as a great drought, volcanic eruption, flooding, or an earthquake. Something traumatic may have forced them to suddenly transition from sedentary farmers and fishermen into nomads.

The Mexica reported that when they left Aztlan, their life of ease was replaced by thorns, thistles, sharp rocks, snakes, and poisonous lizards in a land turned against them. This characterizes the harsh deserts they migrated through in their long journey to the Valley of Mexico. It also provides further hints to the location of Aztlan as being a fertile place but close to desert areas. The northwestern terrain of Mexico is mostly arid or semi-arid, but swathes of tropical wetlands extend up the western part of the country toward the northern border.

La Quemada Pyramid overlooking lake

Marisol Narváez Quiroz[xxix]

One proposed location for Aztlan (or for Chicomoztoca) is La Quemada, an archeological site in the Chichimeca lands in the state of Zacatecas, about 450 miles northwest of Mexico City. Some say the ruins there are from the mysterious Chicomoztoc culture. La Quemada, with a view of a large lake to its east, is on a high hill with trees and green grass, overlooking the desert. Friar Juan de

Torquemada, in his *Monarquía Indiana* (Indian Monarchy), recorded that La Quemada was a stopping-off place for the Aztecs in their migration to the Valley of Mexico. He said the Aztecs stayed there for nine years, then left their elderly people and children there and continued their migration.

La Quemada site, AD 300-1200

La Quemada, the city on a hill, has masonry construction of terraces, statuesque pillars, a majestic pyramid standing 40 feet high, a ball court, and a residential site. The pyramid is unique in that most Mesoamerican pyramids are formed by a core of rubble and packed earth held in place with retaining walls faced with limestone-covered adobe bricks. The La Quemada votive pyramid is solid and much steeper than other Mexican pyramids, albeit smaller.

It's rather surprising to find a site with such grand architecture in the wilderness this far north. What was this sophisticated city doing out in Chichimeca territory, so far from the Valley of Mexico? Archeological evidence suggests La Quemada was not influenced by the Mesoamerican civilizations to the south, such as the Toltec, but built by a people who independently developed their own techniques and styles.

La Quemada[xxx]

Radiocarbon dating places the construction as beginning in AD 300 and extending to 1200. This would place the earlier history of the city long before the Toltec culture but would coincide with when the Aztecs lived in Aztlan and with the time they said they left their island around AD 1168. La Ciudad Quemada means *burnt city*, because the ruins show evidence of a massive fire that apparently destroyed the city. La Quemada has some similarities to the Chalchihuites culture that flourished about 100 miles west of La Quemada from about AD 100 – 1250.

Items that make La Quemada a possible fit with Aztlan include the age of the city, its situation on a high hill in a fertile area surrounded by desert, the pyramid, and destruction by a fire that may have precipitated a migration at about the same time the Mexica left Aztlan. It's not an island in a lake, but a lake is within view. That lake was formed by damming a river on the eastern side of the city. Along the western side of the hill is a jagged ravine, probably a stream bed. Perhaps, centuries ago, before the dam was built, the city was a sort of island surrounded by the river and stream. Alternatively, maybe La Quemada was not Aztlan itself but Chicomóztoc, which, by Friar Torquemada's account, was an area near Aztlan where the Aztecs stopped to regroup, staying nine years before their migration south.

Another clue for the location of Aztlan is the name *Colhuacan* for the great hill on the island of Aztlan. Colhuacan (or *Culhuacan)* is also the name of a pre-Colombian city-state founded by the Toltecs under Mixcoatl (and remember Mixcoatl is also supposed to be an ancestor to the Mexica). It is believed to be the first settlement of the Toltecs in the area, even before they built Tula. Colhuacan was in the Valley of Mexico on the shores of Lake Xochimilco, which connected to Lake Texcoco, where the Mexica later established their city of Tenochtitlan on an island. Colhuacan was also known for having floating gardens. It survived the fall of Tula and continued into the Aztec era.

In the Colhuacan region is a hill called Chapultepec (meaning grasshopper) located on an island in Lake Texcoco, close to where the Mexica-Aztec capital city of Tenochtitlan was built. When the Mexica first arrived in the Valley of Mexico, it was populated by the remnant of the Toltecs, by the Chichimeca who had migrated there earlier, by other tribes from Aztlan, and by other cultures. There wasn't much room for the Mexica, and the local people didn't like these newcomers.

However, after years of subservience to other cultures and struggling to survive, the Aztecs managed to take control of Chapultepec, an island on the west side of Lake Texcoco. In the center of this island was a small, extinct volcano rising above a shoreline with freshwater springs. For about twenty years, they lived on this island with a high hill on a lake with the culture of floating gardens. Chapultepec island bore an uncanny resemblance to Aztlan!

Could Chapultepec be the mythical Aztlan? What if the Aztecs were always desert nomads up to this point? What if their life in Aztlan occurred in far more recent history but was "adjusted" in time to build credibility? Alternatively, could later descriptions of Aztlan been clouded by memories of Chapultepec?

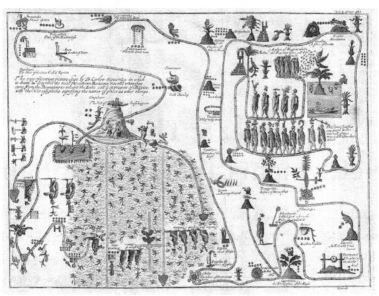

1704 Gemelli Map of the Aztec Migration from Aztlan (upper right corner lake & palm tree) to Chapultepec, in the left middle, a hill with a grasshopper on top)[xxxi]

Even after founding the city of Tenochtitlan, the Mexica had a soft spot in their hearts for Chapultepec Island. It became a sacred place for them, where they built a religious center and a retreat for their emperors. The hill on the island is believed to be where the ashes of cremated Aztec emperors were buried.

Was Aztlan real or mythical? This is a mystery for which we have no definite answer. Were the Aztecs always hunters and gathers before settling in Tenochtitlan, or did they have origins as agriculturalists? We can glean clues from their legends, from archeology, and from linguistics, yet the beginnings of the people that would build a great empire are shrouded in mist.

Chapter 5: The Early Settlements and Tenochtitlan

Assuming Aztlan was a real place, one can imagine the disorientation and ·bewilderment of the Mexica-Aztecs when they left their ancestral home. Some cataclysmic event, perhaps warfare or natural disaster or the voice of their god, had forced the exile. What would happen to them? Where would they go?

According to their own accounts, they were soon comforted by the singing of the hummingbird god Huitzilopochtli, who told them he had adopted them as his people and would lead them to a new home. He promised them he would provide them with the tools they needed for their journey and that they would be great and prosperous. In return, he demanded sacrifice, gory sacrifice.

A hummingbird seems a strange manifestation for a deity who was the god of war and the god of the sun. Huitzilopochtli's name literally meant *hummingbird of the left (left was south to the Mexica)*. The Mexica believed that warriors were reincarnated as hummingbirds. Night after night, this reincarnated warrior Huitzilopochtli sang to them, instructing them where to go and what to do.

After the Mexica-Azteca crossed the lake from Aztlan, they encountered the other tribes who, like the Mexica, had each come out of the seven caves of Aztlan: the Xochimilca, Tlahuica, Acolhua, Tlaxcalteca, Tepaneca, and Chalca. These tribes, who had left Aztlan earlier, asked to join the Mexica, and they journeyed together for some time.

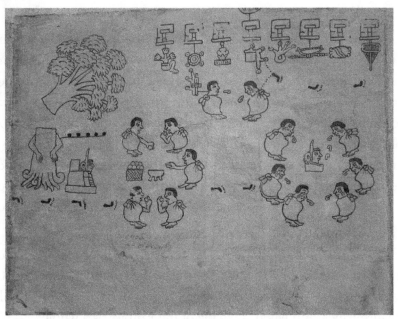

Broken tree, a symbol of the split of the Mexica from other Aztec tribes. To the right of the picture, six men are gathered around Huitzilopochtli, pictured as a man in a hummingbird mouth. From the Codex Boturini.[xxii]

After arriving at a place called Tlatzallan Texcaltepetzallan, the Mexica's god Huitzilopochtli ordered them to separate from the other tribes; this division is pictured in the *Codex Boturini* as the top of a tree cut off from the trunk. Over 100 years later, the Mexica did meet up again with their kinsmen Aztec tribes from Aztlan, who got to the Valley of Mexico before them. The other Aztec tribes did not give the Mexica a warm welcome.

Following their separation from the other tribes, their god announced that they were now to be called Mexica, not Aztec. The people we know today as Aztecs mostly called themselves Mexica throughout their history. The name Aztec was an inclusive term for all the seven tribes from the seven caves of Aztlan. This can get confusing because in more recent history, the Mexica tribe has often been called *Aztec*.

Today, the term *Aztec* is sometimes used exclusively for the Mexica tribe who eventually settled in Tenochtitlan. The name *Aztec* is more accurately used to designate the three main tribes of the Triple Alliance who formed the Aztec Empire: the Mexica, Acolhua, and Tepanec. These three tribes all came from Aztlan, so collectively, they are correctly called Aztec. The name *Aztec* also can refer to all the citizens of the city-states that were loosely part of the Empire and spoke Nahuatl as a common language. Many tribes of these city-states were among the seven tribes from Aztlan, so of Aztec heritage.

For clarity, this book uses the term *Mexica* or *Mexica-Aztec* when referring to the specific tribe that settled Tenochtitlan. It uses *Aztec* when speaking of the seven tribes of Aztlan, the Triple Alliance tribes, and when speaking of the Empire as a whole.

First Human Sacrifice by Mexica, as depicted in Codex Boturini.[xxxiii]

Getting back to the long migration, the Mexica remained under the broken tree for four years after their breakup with the other Aztec tribes. It is at this point that they began the grisly practice of human sacrifice. The *Codex Boturini* depicts Huitzilopochtli guiding them through the slaughter of three victims, two men and a woman of the Chicomóztoc-Mimixcoa tribe. In this picture, you can see the fourth man from the left carrying the hummingbird god Huitzilopochtli on his back; the god has the head of a bird with a long beak combined with a human head.

The *Crónica Mexicayotl* says that the Mexica-Aztecs continued journeying south, living off the land for many decades. They would stop for a season when they came to a more fertile place, remaining long enough to plant and then harvest a crop, which they could carry with them. This indicates that the Mexica were not completely hunters and gatherers; they must have had an agricultural background to know how to grow crops.

Huitzilopochtli's sister Malinalxoch was traveling with them, a beautiful sorceress who dealt in witchcraft with snakes, scorpions, and other poisonous creatures. Huitzilopochtli thought his sister was evil – incongruous, as he was the one commanding his followers to rip the hearts out of living people as tribute to him. He warned the Mexica that she was a grave threat to them.

"Sorcery is not my way," Huitzilopochtli explained. "My way is war."

Huitzilopochtli went on to tell them the rewards of their conquest under his guidance: "This will bring us jade, gold and colored feathers to decorate my temple. You will have corn and chocolate and cotton. Together, we will have everything."

One day while the sorceress was sleeping, Huitzilopochtli and the Mexica quietly crept away, leaving her behind. Years later, Malinalxoch's son Copil attempted to avenge the abandonment of his mother by attacking the Mexica in their cherished island of Chapultepec. That did not go well for Copil. The Mexica killed him, and following Huitzilopochtli's instructions, cut out his heart and threw it into Lake Texcoco. Mexica myth says that the island that would later become Tenochtitlan grew from Copil's heart.

After decades of nomadic wandering, the Mexica arrived at Tula (Tollan), the ghost town of the Toltecs. They walked about Tula's dramatic ruins, learning from the remaining locals of how the Toltecs ruled the area. They settled in Tula for twenty years, perhaps scheming how they would one day establish an empire of their own. Later, when they arrived in the Valley of Anahuac (Valley of Mexico), they would seek alliances with the Colhuacan people, a branch of the Toltecs, intermarrying with them to establish a Toltec lineage.

Following their twenty-year sojourn in the ruins of Tula, the Mexica resumed their migration south, entering the Valley of Anahuac sometime around AD 1220 to 1240. The new world they encountered was an advanced civilization, more densely populated than what they'd experienced before and politically organized into city-states. Fertile soil and dependable rainfall promoted extensive agriculture, primarily of corn.

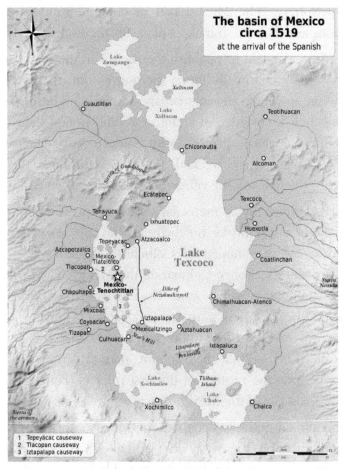

Location of major city-states around Lake Texcoco.[xxxiv]

Who was there, in the Valley of Anahuac, when they arrived? They encountered four of the Aztec tribes they'd split off from over a century before: the Xochimilca, Acolhua, Tepaneca, and Chalca. Their kinsmen and other people in the valley shunned them, not wanting competition for the land, the resources, and the political power each group was striving to build.

The powerful Colhuacan-Toltecs ruled the southern part of the valley, and the Tepanec city of Azcapotzalco was rapidly forming an empire to the west. Other Chichimec tribes had migrated in, living in the periphery. The Mexica had to contend with these other civilizations as they tried to make a place for themselves.

The Mexica sought to establish themselves in the mainstream of the active valley culture by hiring themselves out as stone cutters, construction workers, and mercenary soldiers. These vocations enhanced their knowledge of architecture and honed their military skill. They initiated alliances with various city-states through marriage. Finally, they worked toward establishing their own settlements; the first was the village of Huixachtitlan, settled in 1240.

Their employment as mercenary warriors proved immediately beneficial when war broke out between the *altepetl* (city-state) of Tenayocan and the altepetl of Colhuacan. Seeking to ingratiate themselves with the Toltec Colhuacan, the Mexica allied with them to successfully fight Tenayocan. Having won the favor of the Colhuacan, they formed a marriage alliance by giving a young woman from one of their noble families to marry a prince of Colhuacan. This couple had a son named Coxcoxtli, whose daughter became the mother of the first ruler of Tenochtitlan, the eventual capital city of the Mexica-Aztec.

As mentioned in the last chapter, the Mexica captured the island of Chapultepec on the west side of Lake Texcoco, essentially establishing it as an independent city-state. Their life on this beloved island ended in about twenty years, when several other city-states attacked them, enraged by their audacity to establish an independent city amid their territory. The Tepanec won the war, expelled the Mexica from Chapultepec, and captured the Mexica leader Huehue Huitzilihuitl and his daughter to be human sacrifices to their gods.

The Mexica who survived the battle hid in the marshes around the lake but eventually had to come out to survive. They surrendered to Colhuacan, offering themselves as slaves in return for protection from the Tepanec. As it turns out, the Colhuacan leader was Coxcoxtli, son of the Mexica princess who had married a Colhuacan prince. He gave them permission to settle in Tizapan, an empty, barren land. The Mexica lived there for a few years, assimilating the Colhuacan culture.

Following a grotesque incident in 1303, the Mexica were exiled from Colhuacan. The series of events leading up to the gruesome scene began when the Colhuacan went to war with the Xochimilca, who had built a powerful altepetl to the south of Colhuacan territory. The Xochimilca were Aztec kinsmen of the Mexica from Aztlan; however, the Mexica threw their lot in with the Colhuacan, led by their kinsman Coxcoxtli.

According to the *Codex Aubin*, the Colhuacan were losing, so King Coxcoxtli called on the Mexica: "Go to the Xochimilca who are defeating us and capture 8000 of them to be our slaves," he commanded.

The Mexica requested shields and clubs for this endeavor, but the king refused, so the Mexica set off on their mammoth task. Ever the overachievers, instead of capturing the Xochimilca, they killed them – and not just 8000; they kept on going and killed 32,000! They cut the noses off the warriors, filled their sacks with them, and marched back to King Coxcoxtli.

"O ruler, here are all our captives. We caught 32,000 of them." They dropped the bloody bags full of noses in front of Coxcoxtli.

Horrified, Coxcoxtli called for his advisors. "The Mexica are not human! How did they do this to the Xochimilca? They are a bad omen!"

The Mexica pressed their advantage, "O Ruler, give our earth altar a little something to adorn it."

They wanted Coxcoxtli's daughter; they wanted to worship her as a goddess, they said. Perhaps the Colhuacan king had misgivings, but he gave them his daughter to be worshiped as a goddess. When the king arrived for the ceremony, one of the Mexica priests was strolling around in the skin of his daughter! She had been killed and flayed, and he was wearing her! As can be expected, the Mexica's macabre perspective of how to worship a goddess incited a terrible battle and the Mexica's expulsion from Colhuacan. They then had to wander through the swamps and lake areas as outcasts.

At first, they tried to settle north of Colhuacan, in Mexicaltzingo. But their horrific reputation had preceded them, and the people of that area forced them to keep going. They finally found an island called Nextipac, on the shores of Lake Texcoco, where they settled for a while. But the Colhuacan, their one-time allies turned enemies, attacked them there, burning down their town, leaving no trace that Nextipac had ever existed.

The Mexica fled; using their shields as rafts, they paddled away and hid out among the reeds of the lake edge. The Mexica had lost many of their people, all their belongings, and now they were hiding in the swamp, with the Colhuacan pressing down on them. They were in a desperate situation; what would save them now?

That night, the hummingbird god, Huitzilopochtli, appeared in a dream to one of the tribal leaders: "When morning comes, get up and seek a prickly-pear cactus, standing among the reeds. On it, an eagle will be perched, eating a snake. Here you must build your city, Tenochtitlan. And here you must await your surrounding enemies and conquer them, one by one, all of them."

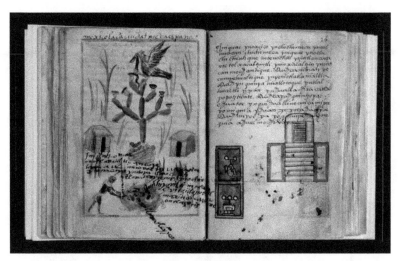

Eagle on cactus eating a snake, from Codex Aubin folio 25[xxxv]

The next morning, the tribal elder called the people together and told him of the prophecy he had received in his dream. The people set off, looking over their shoulders in case the Colhuacan were still following. Their eyes scanned the area, searching among the reeds, an unlikely place for a cactus to grow. And then, on a marshy island on the western shore of Lake Texcoco, they saw an eagle, spreading his wings and perched on a prickly pear cactus growing in the reeds! It was eating a snake it held in its talons.

Eagle on cactus with bird, from the 16th century Tovar Codex.[xxxvi]

(Some earlier versions of the story don't include the snake – just the eagle and the cactus. They show the eagle eating the cactus fruit or eating a bird. It's possible the snake might have entered the story after the Spanish arrived, perhaps by mistranslating the Mexica writings.)

This was the place! After all those years of wandering, of fighting the elements, struggling to survive, longing for a place to call home, here it was! Here was the island where they would build their city Tenochtitlan. It was the year AD 1325. They had left their island home of Aztlan in 1168, and after the long migration had finally come to their new island home.

Building their new city in the middle of a swampy area may have seemed inauspicious beginnings. And yet, this low-lying island on a lake was a strategic location. They would have plenty of food from fish and waterfowl and from farming where there was a constant source of water. Lake Texcoco was connected to other lakes, providing multiple waterways for trade, transportation, and setting out on war expeditions.

Of course, they didn't own the island. It was under the control of the *tlatoani* (king) of the city of Azcapotzalco, the seat of the Tepanec Empire. The Tepanec were the Mexica's kinsmen from Aztlan and one-time allies, but more recently, their enemies. Would the Tepanec king permit them to live there? Yes! In exchange for becoming vassals of Azcapotzalco and mercenary warriors for the Tepanec, they could stay!

All they had to do was fight with the Tepanec against the other altepetls, especially Colhuacan and Texcoco, the city-state of the Acolhua, also kinsmen from Aztlan. Together, the Mexica and the Tepanec defeated Colhuacan and Texcoco, bringing all the territories around Lake Texcoco under the control of the Tepanec Empire. With the area secured, the Mexica could now turn their focus to building their city.

In 1375, Tenoch, their esteemed chieftain of the long migration, died. After their period of mourning, the Mexica gathered to decide who would be the next leader of their fledgling city. It would have to be someone who would command the respect of the surrounding city-states and have ties with the political elite of the region. Nobody in their own group met the criteria, so they started looking further afield, at Colhuacan, of all places.

So, yes, there was that gruesome incident where their priest had dressed himself in the skin of the Colhuacan princess, leading to their exile. And yes, they had allied with the Tepanec to defeat

Colhuacan and bring it under Tepanec control. But through their intermarriages with the Colhuacan royals, they had developed important blood ties.

Remember, Coxcoxtli himself was the son of a Mexica princess. Coxcoxtli's daughter, Atotoztli (not the one who was skinned), had married Opochtli Iztahuatzin, a Mexica leader, and given birth to a son named Acamapichtli. This boy was of Mexica lineage but also of Colhuacan royalty – and was related to the Acolhua tribe as well. Through his Colhuacan bloodline, he was a descendent of the Toltecs. The Mexica elders could not think of a better candidate with ties to all the right people to be their next ruler.

Acamapichtli, the first Aztec King (Reigned 1376-1395). From Tovar Codex.[xxxvii]

A delegation headed to Texcoco to invite Acamapichtli to be their governor, and he accepted! The young man of twenty came to Tenochtitlan in 1376, greeted with much pageantry. Acamapichtli solidified ties with the Colhuacan by marrying the daughter of the king and then affirmed his standing in his new city by marrying three Mexica women, each from one of the three major houses of

Tenochtitlan. The Aztec-Mexica dynasty was now established. Soon, it would grow into multiple city-states and eventually into a great Mesoamerican empire.

Chapter 6: Aztec City-States

For the next fifty years, through canny politics, warfare, and astute alliances, the fierce Mexica rose to prominence, establishing themselves as a political power with dominance over several other city-states. During the reign of their first three kings, they focused on consolidating their own city-state of Tenochtitlan while expanding its size and embarking on massive architectural projects. They also began to take possession of smaller city-states which would pay tribute money, serve as allies against enemy forces, and provide a source of trade. In this chapter, we will explore how they began acquiring these city-states and how the city-states were organized and related to each other.

The Mexica city of Tenochtitlan was developing in a larger Mesoamerican culture that focused on extensive agriculture combined with complex, densely populated urban centers. These large cities served as the religious, political, and economic centers for the surrounding population. Most of these urban areas formed alliances with other cities; the smaller, weaker cities became tributaries to the larger, more powerful cities. The tributaries would provide goods and services, including mercenary soldiers, along with tribute payments to their overlords.

Mexica warriors: Eagle Warrior at the left and Jaguar Warrior at the right brandishing a macuahuitl (a wooden club with sharp obsidian blades). From the Florentine Codex.[xxxviii]

In the case of Tenochtitlan, the Mexica were initially allies and tributaries to the Tepanec city of Azcapotzalco. Together, these two cities began to rise in power. Through supplying warriors for successful military campaigns, the Mexica enabled Azcapotzalco to evolve into an empire with major regional power. The Tepanec emperor Tezozomoc greatly appreciated the support from Tenochtitlan and began granting the Mexica part of the tribute as they conquered other city-states together. Eventually, Tenochtitlan became a city-state in its own right.

In the political system of that day, a *tlatoani* was king of a city-state, and a *Huey Tlatoani* was the ruler of a city-state that had other cities as tributaries under it (something like an emperor over an empire). When Acamapichtli was first brought to Tenochtitlan to rule, his status was that of *cihuacóatl* or governor, as Tenochtitlan was still developing into a proper city. In the next seven years, as Tenochtitlan grew in power and in esteem, it was eventually recognized as a city-state (although still a tributary to the Tepanec). In 1382, Acamapichtli was crowned *Tlatoani* (King) of Tenochtitlan, with great fanfare.

While the Tepanec of Azcapotzalco, with their Tenochtitlan allies, were expanding their power base on the western shores of Lake Texcoco, the Acolhua city of Texcoco was developing into a major contender on the northeastern side of the lake. When war broke out between Azcapotzalco and Texcoco, the Mexica fought with their Tepanec allies, and together they conquered Texcoco.

During Acamapichtli's reign, Mexica warriors continued to fight with the Tepanec against other city-states. Eventually, they were permitted to engage in their own expeditions. In these military campaigns, they conquered the Tlahuaca city of Cuauhnahuac and Xochimilco to the south, making them their first tributary states! The Tlahuaca and Xochimilco were two of the seven tribes from Aztlan, so the Mexica were building the Aztec base of power.

The marshy island on which Tenochtitlan was located was expanded during Acamapichtli's reign by hauling in dirt and rock to build up the original island and by building a causeway to a nearby island. As an island city, Tenochtitlan lacked land to grow enough food for the population. Acamapichtli expanded the chinampas (floating gardens) around the city. After Xochimilco became a tributary city, the Xochimilco shipped fruit and vegetables to Tenochtitlan from their own floating gardens in the south.

Illustration of Tenochtitlan showing causeway and Templo Mayor[xxix]

The Mexica began replacing their reed houses with houses of stone, wood, and loam. Acamapichtli developed the city into four districts centered around the great temple complex, which included the *Templo Mayor*, a high pyramid with two temples on top. The *Templo Mayor* was rebuilt numerous times over the coming years, becoming taller each time. The temple complex also had a ball court and a skull rack and was surrounded by the palaces of the elite. Canals throughout the city provided transportation. Anthropologists have estimated that the population of Tenochtitlan at its peak was 200,000.

As a political leader, Acamapichtli shrewdly built up the Mexica's strength through forming alliances with other rival clans rather than fighting them. He kept relations steady with the Tepanec emperor Tezozomoc by promptly paying the demanded tribute. Once, when in Tezozomoc's city of Azcapotzalco, Acamapichtli bought a beautiful woman in the slave market. With this slave, he had a son named Itzcoatl, who became Tlatoani of Tenochtitlan in 1427, after Acamapichtli's older son Huitzilihuitl and his grandson Chimalpopoca reigned as kings of Tenochtitlan.

Acamapichtli died young in his mid-forties. Before his death, he was eager to settle the matter of his successor. The custom of the Mexica was to elect their leaders. The elders would make this decision, and generally, the next ruler was from the royal family, but not necessarily the oldest son. It could be a nephew or some other relative. From his death bed, Acamapichtli summoned the chiefs of the four districts of Tenochtitlan. He advised them he wanted them to continue the custom of electing their leaders.

The four chiefs held a council and elected Acamapichtli's oldest son Huitzilihuitl, who was only sixteen years old. Acamapichtli approved this choice before he died. A discerning young man, Huitzilihuitl knew his detractors might question his election by only four leaders. He ordered a new election with a larger group of priests, elders, and warrior chiefs to cast their votes and won again, solidifying his right to the throne.

Huitzilihuitl assumed the throne in 1395 and ruled until 1417. The Codex Aubin noted that in the year Huitzilihuitl acceded the throne, a swarm of grasshoppers besieged the area, causing a year of famine. He maintained friendly relations with the Tepanec Emperor Tezozomoc of Azcapotzalco, marrying his daughter Ayauhcihuatl. After this, Tezozomoc lowered Tenochtitlan's tribute payments to a nominal level. Huitzilihuitl and Ayauhcihuatl had a son named Chimalpopoca, who became the next tlatoani. Another wife, Miahuaxihuitl, gave birth to Moctezuma I, who later became the *Huey Tlatoani* of the Aztecs (Huey Tlatoani, not just tlatoani, as by that time Tenochtitlan was an empire).

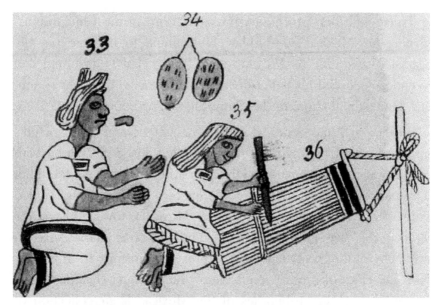

Mother teaching daughter to weave cotton[xl]

A wise leader, Huitzilihuitl continued his father's policies of brokering peaceful alliances with neighboring states. During his reign, cotton weaving became an important industry. Previously, the people had worn clothing made from maguey (agave) fiber, which was scratchy, like burlap. Now they could wear soft and cool cotton, which could be dyed in the bright colors the Mexica loved. The cotton industry was so productive that they exported cotton to Azcapotzalco and to Cuauhnahuac, their vassal city in the far south.

When the ruler of the city of Texcoco died in 1409, his son Ixtlixochitl became tlatoani and quickly began challenging the status quo. The Mexica's involvement in this was complicated. Decades earlier, they had allied with the Tepanec in a war against Texcoco and won. At that time, Texcoco had become a tributary city to Azcapotzalco. The new ruler Ixtlixochitl continued paying tribute to the Tepanec city, but when Emperor Tezozomoc of Azcapotzalco offered his daughter in marriage to him, he chose Huitzilihuitl's daughter Matlalcihuatzin instead.

Ixtlixochitl then proclaimed himself "Lord of the Chichimeca," inviting his Mexica father-in-law Huitzilihuitl to become his ally against Tezozomoc of Azcapotzalco. That meant Huitzilihuitl had to choose between his father-in-law Tezozomoc and his new son-in-law. Huitzilihuitl chose his long-time ally Tezozomoc.

Angry at the snub to his daughter and Ixtlixochitl's insubordination, Emperor Tezozomoc led his army, along with Mexica warriors, to attack Texcoco. After two years, the joint Tepanec and Mexica forces conquered Texcoco and killed Ixtlixochitl. As a reward for the Mexica's loyalty, Emperor Tezozomoc gave Texcoco to Tenochtitlan as a tributary. Texcoco was a city of the Acolhua tribe, the Mexica's kinsmen from Aztlan. Now the cities of three Aztec tribes – the Acolhua, Tlahuaca, and Xochimilco – were tributaries of the Mexica. Their collection of city-states was growing!

Like his father, Huitzilihuitl died young, at only 38. His son Chimalpopoca, age twenty, assumed the throne in 1417 and ruled until 1427, only ten years. One of his achievements was fulfilling his father's dream of an aqueduct to bring fresh water into Tenochtitlan. Even though they were on an island in a lake, thermal springs around the island made the water saline. The connecting lakes and other parts of Lake Texcoco were fed by freshwater springs, so the Mexica had to get drinking water from there or from the mainland. Chimalpopoca's maternal grandfather, Emperor Tezozomoc of Azcapotzalco, assisted with the project of constructing a wooden aqueduct from Chapultepec to Tenochtitlan. Chimalpopoca also built a causeway to Tlacopan on the mainland, with bridges that could be lifted at night or when threatened by invasion.

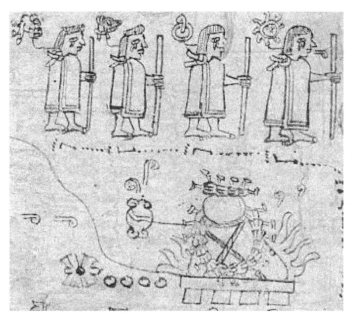

Funeral pyre of Emperor Tezozomoc, from the Codex Xolotl[di]

Intrigue surrounded Chimalpopoca's death when he was only thirty. Was it suicide or an assassination associated with a coup d'état? His grandfather Tezozomoc, the Tepanec Emperor, died in 1427. Tezozomoc's son, Tayatzin, Chimalpopoca's uncle on his mother's side, succeeded his father. Within days, Tayatzin's older brother Maxtla staged a rebellion and stole the throne. Chimalpopoca joined forces with Tayatzin to retake the throne of Azcapotzalco. Tayatzin was killed in the struggle, and warriors from Azcapotzalco invaded Tenochtitlan, captured Chimalpopoca, and took him back to Azcapotzalco, where he was placed in a cage. He either committed suicide by hanging himself with his belt, or he was strangled by his Tepanec captors.

However, some scholars believe his death was at the hands of his Mexica uncle Itzcoatl, who succeeded him as ruler of Tenochtitlan. They say Itzcoatl was the undercover leader of a secret rebel force that had been plotting against their overlords and long-time allies, the Tepanec. As the grandson of Tezozomoc, who had generously helped with the aqueduct and in other ways, Chimalpopoca was loyal to the Tepanec. These scholars believed he was secretly assassinated by his uncle Itzcoatl, and his death blamed on the Tepanec.

Regardless of how Chimalpopoca died, the saga between Tenochtitlan and Azcapotzalco continued, ending in the Triple Alliance, which we will cover in the next chapter. For now, let's review more about the city-state culture in the Valley of Mexico to better understand the development of the Aztec Empire.

The Mexica-Aztecs began to grow into an empire through military conquest, trade, and forming valuable alliances. They installed friendly rulers in territories they conquered and intermarried with the ruling dynasties. The *altepetl* or city-states that came under their control were generally able to retain their own leaders and religion, but they had to support the growing Mexica Empire and the tlatoani of Tenochtitlan through tribute payments. They also had to include the Mexica god, Huitzilopochtli, in the worship of their deities. Failure to comply would result in the Mexica military attacking their city and destroying temples and other buildings. Needless to say, this created resentment in some of their tributary cities.

The altepetl (city-states) of the growing Mexica-Aztec empire were organized in a hierarchal system. Each altepetl had its own tlatoani (king) who ruled over the nobles and commoners in his territory. Each city-state had its own capital, which was the trade hub and center for religious activity, around which were spread the agricultural lands and smaller towns and villages.

Most city-states were marked by one specific ethnic identity, although they were all multi-ethnic with several spoken languages. The *lingua-franca* (common language) for all the city-states under Mexica control was Nahuatl, the language group of Aztec tribes as well the Chichimeca tribes and the descendants of the Toltec Empire.

The word *tlatoani* for the ruler of the city-states literally means *one who speaks*, indicating that he was a representative for his people. The tlatoani was not only the political leader but usually also the high priest and commander-in-chief for his city-state. He was considered the owner of all the lands in the altepetl and would receive tribute from these lands and smaller towns and villages. He supervised the markets and temples and served as a judge to resolve disputes brought from the high court. Under the tlatoani was his second-in-command, the *cihuacōātl,* who served as the chief judge of the court system and appointed lower court judges. The cihuacōātl was also the chief financial officer for the tlatoani.

Most tlatoani were of royal blood but usually elected from a pool of four candidates by a council of nobles, warriors, and priests. Once elected, the tlatoani served for life and was permitted to have multiple wives, which generated many children to continue his legacy.

Four Aztec warriors, from the Codex Mendoza[xlii]

Whenever a city-state was defending its territory or involved in a military campaign against other city-states, the tlatoani, as commander-in-chief, would create war strategies for his military force. He would base this on information he received from scouts, spies, and messengers who assessed the situation at the rival city-state regarding the position of the enemy and points of strength and weakness. He would be informed immediately of the success or failure of skirmishes and any deaths or captives. The tlatoani would also rally support from friendly city-states, sending gifts and requesting their help.

The commoners in the smaller towns and villages surrounding the capital city of a city-state were subdivided into smaller units called *calpolli.* Each calpolli would have a *tecutli* (landlord) who would govern that region and distribute the land among the commoners, who usually were kinspeople related through intermarriage. The tecutli or landlord might be of commoner origin but usually rose to nobility status as a representative of his calpolli to the higher authorities.

The farmers did not own their own land; it was more of a feudal land system where farmers would pay tribute to their landlord in the form of a portion of their crops from the land assigned to them, and tradespeople would pay tribute from their manufactured goods like cotton cloth and clothing articles, baskets, pottery, tools, and even paper! Archeologists estimate that a typical altepetl had 10,000 to 15,000 residents in an area of around 30 to 40 square miles.

The Mexica discouraged connections among their tributary city-states, limiting communication and trade between the city-states, preferring them to be dependent on Tenochtitlan as their major trade partner. This made Tenochtitlan more powerful as the major trade center for the Lake Texcoco region. It also helped secure Mexica power. If the city-states started interacting with each other, becoming friendly and trading and intermarrying, this could lead to them forming allies and potentially challenging their Mexica-Aztec overlords.

Each altepetl was its own political unit, separate from the other city-states. Warfare was common between the city-states who were tributaries to the Mexica-Aztec, especially if one was a Nahuatl-speaking tribe and the other was of some other ethnicity.

The Mexica-Aztec continued conquering other Mesoamerican city-states and expanding their empire. In 1430, the Triple Alliance formed between three powerful cities – Tenochtitlan, Texcoco, and Tlacopan (as we will cover in the next chapter). At that point, the lands that had once been part of the Tepanec Empire were divided between the three cities, so each gained more territory. The Mexica-Aztec Empire ruled most of the city-states around Lake Texcoco, including Azcapotzalco, Colhuacan, Chapultepec, Coyoacan, Chalca, Tenayuca, and Xochimilco.

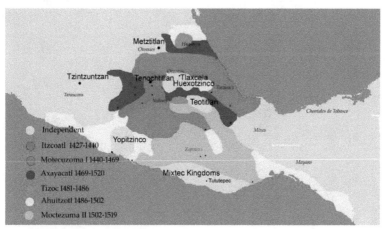

Expansions by various Mexica-Aztec rulers.[xliii]

Following the formation of the Triple Alliance, the empire continued expansion into areas outside the Valley of Mexico, acquiring Huaxtepec, to the south, in what is now the state of Morelos, and Oaxaca even further south. They conquered Tlaxcala and Cholula in the Pueblo Valley. The empire eventually stretched from the Pacific Ocean to the Gulf of Mexico and as far south as

Guatemala. Tenochtitlan ruled over approximately 500 small city-states with up to six million people spanning over 80,000 square miles. When the nomadic Mexica dreamed of ruling an empire, they probably never envisioned how extensive it would one day become.

Chapter 7: The Triple Alliance

His name meant *obsidian snake*, an apt description for the fourth tlatoani of Tenochtitlan. Obsidian was the black volcanic glass the Chichimeca used for arrows, so sharp it penetrated the chainmail armor of the Spaniards. Itzcoatl was like a snake, unnoticed in the grass until the opportunity came for a lethal strike.

His father was Acamapichtli, the first tlatoani of Tenochtitlan. But Itzcoatl was a younger son, and his mother was a slave. While his half-brother Huitzilihuitl reigned, and then when Huitzilihuitl's son Chimalpopoca reigned, Itzcoatl remained in the shadows, quietly forming alliances with other royal sons from nearby cities – the younger sons, born from unimportant wives or concubines. As he secretly plotted his rebellion against the Mexica's Tepanec overlords, Itzcoatl sought out alliances with leading families from Tlacopan and Texcoco, small city-states oppressed by Azcapotzalco.

The chaos following the death of the Tepanec Emperor Tezozomoc gave Itzcoatl the chance to maneuver the situation to his advantage. While Tezozomoc's heirs engaged in a desperate struggle for the Tepanec throne, the mysterious death of Itzcoatl's nephew Chimalpopoca opened the door for Itzcoatl to assume the Mexica throne. Itzcoatl's successful power play eventually resulted in the downfall of Azcapotzalco, the most powerful city in the Valley of Mexico. When Azcapotzalco fell, the Aztec Empire was born.

Events leading up to the great battle of Azcapotzalco began with a coup d'état in the Tepanec city of Azcapotzalco, with Maxtla wresting the throne from his brother. Days after, in Tenochtitlan, Itzcoatl became tlatoani. The two cities had been strong allies since the founding of Tenochtitlan, with the Mexica aiding Azcapotzalco's rise as the strongest city-state in the Valley of Mexico. Tenochtitlan was technically a tributary city to Azcapotzalco, but the former emperor had reduced the tribute payments to a nominal amount out of gratitude for the Mexica's loyal support.

Now, Maxtla, the new Tepanec *Huey Tlatoani*, blockaded Tenochtitlan, cut off their freshwater supply, and demanded higher tribute payments. The Alcoa city of Texcoco was also victimized by Maxtla's despotic demands. Texcoco's king, Nezahualcoyotl the poet, was half-Alcoa and half-Mexica, the grandson of Huitzilihuitl, second king of Tenochtitlan. Hearing that Maxtla planned to kill him, Nezahualcoyotl fled from Texcoco. While in exile, he had an epiphany, which was recorded later by his great-grandson Juan Bautista Pomar:

> "Truly the gods I worship are idols that do not speak nor feel . . . some immensely powerful and unknown god is the creator of the whole universe. He is the only one that can console me in my affliction and help me in such anguish as my heart feels; I want him to be my helper and protection."

Nezahualcoyotl (1402-1472), ruler of Texcoco, from the Codex Ixtlilxochitl.[xliv]

Once Nezahualcoyotl regained power in Texcoco, he built a pyramid and wrote hymns to the *unknown God of everywhere, life giver and peerless One*. But that day had not yet come. At the moment, Nezahualcoyotl needed to rally support for his city. He found an ally in the Toltec-Chichimeca city of Huexotzinco, far to the east. Their king agreed to assist Nezahualcoyotl in his struggle against Maxtla.

Meanwhile, Itzcoatl, already friendly with Texcoco and Huexotzinco, was calling in support from another friend, the tlatoani of Tlacopan. Tlacopan was a small Tepanec city that belonged to the city-state of Azcapotzalco, but they had supported the losing side in the civil war for succession in Azcapotzalco. Fearing the wrath of Maxtla, they decided to join forces with Itzcoatl and the Mexica of Tenochtitlan.

Nezahualcoyotl, realizing several city-states were preparing to resist Maxtla and Azcapotzalco, brilliantly envisioned a coalition forming a massive military force to take down the ferocious and mighty Tepanec empire. This alliance consisted of Tenochtitlan, Texcoco, Huexotzinco, Tlacopan, and Tlatelolco (a small Mexica sister-city just next to Tenochtitlan). Over 100,000 warriors formed the coalition army in 1428 to gain ascendency over the Tepanec bastion of Azcapotzalco.

The army formed three divisions which won back three of the Acolhua cities of the kingdom of Texcoco: Otumba and Acolman to the north, and Coatlinchan to the south. Now Nezahualcoyotl marched to his own city of Texcoco and defeated the Tepanec, while another division gained control over Acolhuacan. Once most towns and cities of the kingdom of Texcoco were secured, Nezahualcoyotl reclaimed his crown while the coalition continued to attack isolated Tepanec posts.

Battle of Azcapotzalco, from Tovar Codex, with jaguar warriors and other fighters. To the right, a priest is sacrificing a small child while two other victims lie on the ground.[xlv]

The coalition warriors then turned to the western shores of Lake Texcoco toward the Tepanec capital of Azcapotzalco. After a siege of 112 days, they overthrew the great city, burning it down and massacring the population. The Tepanec empire, to which they had all been tributary cities, was finally conquered. This turned the three main players, Tenochtitlan, Texcoco, and Tlacopan, into independent city-states. Through seizing power in a coordinated coup d'état, they won freedom for themselves and went on to exert massive power over central Mexico for nearly 100 years. Out of this coalition, the Triple Alliance would be born.

Once the Tepanec Empire was overthrown, the warriors of Huexotzinco returned to their home in the east. The three major powers – the Mexica city of Tenochtitlan, the Acolhua city of Texcoco, and the Tepanec city of Tlacopan – formed a treaty called the Triple Alliance. All three of these tribes were part of the original seven tribes from the caves of Aztlan. These Aztec tribes gave birth to the Aztec Empire, which would soon extend from the Pacific Ocean to the Gulf of Mexico.

The lands of the Tepanec Empire were divided between the three conquering cities. Part of their agreement was to continue conquering other cities with the coalition army. The new lands they acquired would be jointly held by all three cities. Tribute from conquered cities was to be divided into one-fifth for Tlacopan and two-fifths each for Tenochtitlan and Texcoco. Each of the three kings of the alliance would take turns serving as the *Huey Tlatoani* (emperor) of the consolidated empire, temporarily holding legal power over the other two.

Triple Alliance Territory, with inset showing the location of three major cities: Tenochtitlan, Texcoco, and Tlacopa. The shaded areas indicate the city-states that paid tribute to the Aztec Empire. Notice that not all the lands were connected; Xoconochco, on the border of Guatemala, was hundreds of miles from other Aztec city-states.[xlvi]

Later that year, the alliance forces conquered Colhuacan and Huitzilopochco. Working to gain control of all city-states in the Lake Texcoco region, the coalition army moved swiftly to conquer Xochimilco and Ixtapalapan in 1430, and Mixquic two years later. The only holdouts were the Chalca, eventually defeated in 1465, and Tlatelolco in 1473.

The primary architect of the Triple Alliance was Itzcoatl's nephew Tlacaelel, a son of King Huitzilihuitl. Tlacaelel was given the title *cihuacōātl*. Now that the city-state of Tenochtitlan had become part of a vast empire, the *Huey Tlatoani* (emperor) served as the executive over external affairs of the empire: war, expansion, tribute, and diplomacy. The *cihuacōātl* managed the internal affairs of the empire and could exercise great influence and power in this position.

Tlacaelel worked diligently to mold the Mexica self-identity as the chosen people called by the god Huitzilopochtli to conquer and rule over other lands. The people of the Aztec Empire worshiped many gods, but Tlacaelel forced the worship of Huitzilopochtli as chief god among all people of the empire. Tlacaelel also endeavored to erase the pre-conquest memories of conquered city-states by burning their historical chronicles. He even burned the chronicles of the Mexica, apparently because they didn't support the narrative of Aztec identity he was seeking to cultivate.

Like other Mesoamerican cultures, human sacrifice had been part of the Mexica culture since they had left Aztlan, but once Tenochtitlan gained dominance in the Triple Alliance, Tlacaelel raised the scale of human sacrifice to horrific numbers to satiate the gods, so the Mexica could maintain power. These daily, large-scale sacrifices demanded victims – lots of victims.

Aztec Warriors, from Florentine Codex[xlvii]

In the past, the Mexica had sacrificed prisoners of war, but they were running out of prisoners once they conquered most of the nearby territories. Consequently, Tlacaelel came up with the idea of *Flower Wars*. These were ritual and regulated wars meant for both sides to capture enough warriors to meet their sacrificial needs. The main enemies of the Aztecs were the Tlaxcala, a people the Aztecs never conquered, along with several other groups from the Pueblo area, including the Cholula. Tlacaelel brokered an agreement between Tenochtitlan and Tlaxcala to engage in a type of warfare where the soldiers would capture rather than kill the enemy soldiers. Once each side had captured enough warriors for sacrifices, the battle would end. These battles would be prearranged by the leaders on both sides every twenty days! The Flower Wars were usually with the Tlaxcala but occasionally with Cholula or other cities.

With a united front, the Triple Alliance rapidly expanded its territory as it conquered one city after another. The Empire's rule over these conquered cities was *hegemonic* (indirect). If the ruler of the city agreed to their demands, he could remain tlatoani and enjoy the protection of the Triple Alliance and the accompanying political stability and enhanced economics. He just needed to pay tribute to the Alliance twice a year and supply warriors for their military campaigns. The conquered cities maintained their local autonomy and conducted their local affairs as before, including their own religions, but they had to add in the Mexica god Huitzilopochtli as their chief deity.

Occasionally, the tlatoani of a conquered city refused to submit to the Triple Alliance requirements. One strategy the Aztecs used with this problem was replacing uncooperative leaders with a governor who was not of the royal family. Another was directly taxing the population and leaving the king out of the equation. A third way was to bribe the tlatoani with tributes from another city far away if he continued to be submissive to the empire. If this sort of persuasion didn't work, and a city continued to fight against the empire or kill their delegates, the Aztecs would destroy the city. This happened to the Huastec people to the east. Because they continued fighting fiercely without surrendering, the allied forces killed most of the people in the area, even the elderly, the children, and the women.

The cities of the Triple Alliance presented a daunting military coalition, but they were also surging economically. Wherever trade relations already existed, they would expand these, with the end effect that the three ruling cities on Lake Texcoco were the center of a trade hub that spread out throughout the Valley of Mexico and beyond. They intermarried within the three ruling states to strengthen their ties and cultivated marriage alliances with the royal families of the cities they conquered.

Once peace was finally achieved in the Lake Texcoco region, each of the three ruling cities of the Empire directed their attention inward to reforming and developing their cities. In Tenochtitlan, schools were built in every neighborhood. Commoners had *telpochcalli* schools, which gave basic instruction in religion and provided boys with military training. The *calmecac* schools were for the nobility and for commoners who seemed promising candidates for the priesthood or as artisans. Laws were passed to clearly define the distinction between nobles and commoners and to grant privileges to warriors and priests. A system of courts and judges was established, with levels of punishment for various crimes.

Dams designed by Nezahualcoyotl for Tenochtitlan.

In Texcoco, Nezahualcoyotl was transforming his city into a cultural center while gaining fame as an engineer and architect. He consulted with the Mexica on the best plans for constructing a bigger aqueduct into Tenochtitlan, using his engineering genius to devise a dam and dike system to control flooding and separate the brackish water from fresh water around Tenochtitlan. In his own city of Texcoco, he built temples and an exquisite palace on the side of a cliff, with an irrigation system to fill his hot tubs overlooking the city.

Hot tubs overlooking the city designed by Nezahualcoyotl.[xlviii]

Nezahualcoyotl was known for gathering *tlamatini* (*someone who knows something*) to Texcoco. These were scholars, sages, astronomists, wisemen, and philosophers – something like the Magi of Persia. Under his leadership, Texcoco blossomed, influencing a cultural renaissance throughout the Aztec Empire.

Nezahualcoyotl disdained the daily blood sacrifices of Tenochtitlan. In 1467, the year one-reed in the Aztec calendar, the great temple of the god Huitzilopochtli was rebuilt and dedicated in Tenochtitlan. As recorded in the *Codex Ixtlilxochitl* by his descendent Fernando de Alva Cortés Ixtlilxochitl, Nezahualcoyotl prophesied: "*In a year such as this, this temple, now new, will be destroyed . . . then the earth will be diminished; the chiefdoms will end.*"

The Aztec calendar was a rotation of 52 reeds or years, so the next year one-reed was 1419. This was the year that Hernán Cortés first entered Tenochtitlan; two years later, the great city fell to the Spaniards.

In his own city of Texcoco, Nezahualcoyotl built a great pyramid, on top of which was a temple, nine stories high, dedicated to *Tloque Nahauque, the unknown god, the uncreated and self-existing creator of all things, life-giver.* He permitted no images or idols and no blood sacrifice; only incense and flowers were offered. At dawn, noon, sunset, and midnight, instruments would play, and Nezahualcoyotl would pray.

Nezahualcoyotl wrote the first codification of law for his city-state, covering property rights, crime, and morality. These eighty comprehensive and concise laws seemed strict and the punishments harsh, but his law code was adopted by other city-states of the Aztec Empire. While Tenochtitlan was burning books and rewriting history, Texcoco was preserving the chronicles of the past, with the death penalty for the willful falsification of historical truth.

Nezahualcoyotl implemented a social welfare system to provide food and clothing for widows, wounded soldiers, and the indigent elderly from the royal treasury, along with school fees for orphans. During the great drought, he provided for his citizens from the treasury, perhaps because he guiltily thought the drought was his fault. Like the Hebrew David and Bathsheba, he had fallen madly in love with the young wife of Cuahcuauhtzin, tlatoani of Tepechpan, one of his minor cities. He sent Cuahcuauhtzin to the frontlines to fight the Tlaxcala, where he was killed; Nezahualcoyotl then claimed Azcalxochitzin as his own wife. Immediately, plagues of locusts and severe drought struck, lasting for three years, which Nezahualcoyotl considered as punishment for his sins.

Coronation of Moctezuma I, Fifth Tlatoani of Tenochtitlan, from the Tovar Codex.[xlix]

Although the three city-states of the Triple Alliance were supposed to be equal partners, Tenochtitlan rose to dominance as its population grew to double that of Texcoco. When Itzcoatl died in 1440, his nephew Moctezuma I assumed the throne of Tenochtitlan, and Nezahualcoyotl traveled to Tenochtitlan to negotiate the continuation of the Triple Alliance. The new terms for the treaty were for Texcoco and Tlacopan to recognize the supremacy of Tenochtitlan.

Nezahualcoyotl arranged a pseudo-battle where his army and the Tenochtitlan warriors met on the battlefield and exchanged insults. Then the Texcoco warriors took off running toward their city with the Mexica warriors in pursuit. At this point, Nezahualcoyotl lit a great fire on top of the primary pyramid of Texcoco, symbolizing his recognition of Tenochtitlan's dominance. Beginning with the reign of Ahuizotl in 1486, the kings of Tenochtitlan were called *Huey Tlatoani* (emperor); the three rulers of the Triple Alliance no longer took turns as the chief leader. The Huey Tlatoani of Tenochtitlan assumed most of the duties of running the Aztec Empire.

Nevertheless, the three cities continued to collaborate in military campaigns to conquer and expand their empire even further. The Purépecha (Tarascan) Empire to the northwest was the nemesis of the Aztec Empire. The Purépecha were expanding their own territory, which sometimes involved claiming lands the Aztecs had already conquered.

When Nezahualcoyotl died in 1472, his son Nezahualpilli assumed the throne of Texcoco; like his father, he was a poet and a seeker of wisdom. After Moctezuma II ascended the throne of Tenochtitlan in 15012, Nezahualpilli warned him that his tlamatini (wisemen) had received a prophecy that foreigners would gain dominion over the Valley of Mexico. Moctezuma was dubious and challenged him to a ball game to test the prophecy. When Moctezuma lost, he feared the omen was true. And so it was. Two years after Nezahualpilli died in 1515, explorer Francisco Hernández de Córdoba landed on the Yucatan coast, the beginning of the end for the Aztec Empire.

Chapter 8: War with the Tarascans

While the Mexica were building Tenochtitlan, another empire was evolving in the high volcanic mountains of the present-day state of Michoacán. Soon it would stretch to Jalisco and Guanajuato, reaching the Pacific Ocean. They never called themselves Tarascans. They were the Purépecha. They were always Purépecha. The word Tarascan came centuries later, from a word for brother-in-law; they used it mockingly for the conquistadors who violated their women. But the Spaniards picked it up and used this epithet for the Purépecha.

Islands of Lake Pátzcuaro

The Purépecha culture appeared in the lake basins of Zacapu, Cuitzeo, and Pátzcuaro around 500 BC, where they settled on islands in the large lakes (yet another island people). A Nahuatl-speaking group joined them several centuries later, bringing a culture of ballcourts and *chac mool* figurines. The Purépecha told the Spanish these people were Toltecs, although some archeologists feel they were Teotihuacan. They may have been escaping a series of volcanic eruptions in central Mexico at that time.

Where did the Purépecha come from? Their origins are puzzling, with a language and culture unlike any others in Mesoamerica. Linguistically, their language is unique, unrelated to Nahuatl or any other languages in Mexico. Some linguists find a possible link to the Zuni of New Mexico and Arizona or the Quechua language of the Incas of South America. Their building style and advanced knowledge of complex metallurgy also hints of Incan influence. Were the Purépecha somehow connected to the people of the South American Andes?

Genetic studies say yes. In 2015, Nicolas Brucato and other researchers presented a study on Native American gene flow between Mesoamerica and the Andes; they found a clear Andean component, albeit minuscule, in the genome of the Purépecha-Tarascans (along with the Maya, Mixtec, and Kaqchiken).

Drawing of a balsa raft near Guayaquil, Ecuador[ii]

In 1526, Spanish explorers described ships or large rafts with cotton sails used by the people of Ecuador and Peru along the Pacific coast, large enough to hold twenty men and carry 25 metric tons. It's conceivable that their trade routes could have extended up the Pacific coast as far north as Mexico. Even though the earlier settlements of the Purépecha were inland, they used the river systems flowing to the Pacific as important trade routes. Scholars believe they may have had contact with South American traders from AD 650 onwards.

Aside from archeological and linguistic studies, our primary knowledge of the Purépecha comes from the *Relación de Michoacán*, a history written in 1540 by the Franciscan priest Fray Jeronimo de Acalá. He translated and recorded accounts from Purépecha nobles of their oral history and traditions. Pictograph manuscripts of their history have also survived, including the *Lienzo de Jucutacuto*.

Coyote statuette attributed to Purépecha-Tarascan culture[lii]

Around AD 1300, a leader arose among the Purépecha-Tarascans named Tariacuri, from the *Wakúsecha* (*warrior eagle*) clan. Tariacuri had a prophetic dream one night: a vision of gathering all the communities around Lake Pátzcuaro into one state, strong and united. He allied with several nearby friendly cities and began systematically conquering cities around the lake, turning them over to his sons and nephews to rule. After Tariacuri died, his son Hiripan continued military campaigns around nearby Lake Cuitzeo.

Unlike the Aztecs, the Purépecha assimilated the cultures of conquered people into their own. In fact, they were so ethnically diverse that the Purépecha were minorities in their own cities. Similar to the Aztecs, the Purépecha instituted a tributary system from the cities they conquered, with tribute paid in the form of laborers, mercenary soldiers, and goods. More and more territories were incorporated into a highly centralized state as they doubled in size. The new territories brought in significant production and trade of farm produce, minerals, and pottery. Everything was centered around their capital city of Tzintzuntzan, which stood distinct from other ancient Mesoamerican cities.

Round yácata pyramids in Tzintzuntzan[liii]

Tzintzuntzan featured astounding and unique monuments and elaborate religious and civic architecture. In the *House of the Wind,* a civic-ceremonial center on a hill overlooking Lake Pátzcuaro, stood five *yácata:* rounded step-pyramids shaped like keyholes. They were covered with fitted stone slabs, like the masonry used by the South American Incas.

By AD 1522, Tzintzuntzan had grown to 35,000 people with a total population around the lake region of 80,000 in 90 towns and cities. As the population grew, extensive terracing projects were carried out on the surrounding mountains to provide land for agriculture. As they conquered the Balsas Basin and Jalisco, the

Purépecha-Tarascans controlled the mining of silver and gold, with skilled craftsmen to work the precious metals. They were the first people of Mexico to use gold and the only ones who used bronze. Their knowledge and crafting of valuable metals was probably the finest in all ancient Mesoamerica. They were the most important producers and traders of tin, bronze, and copper in Mexico.

Map showing Purépecha-Tarascan Empire next to Aztec Empire[liv]

Eventually, the growing empire of the Purépecha came into direct conflict with the Aztec Empire. The two powers were simultaneously expanding, and both were attempting to conquer and incorporate the same territory that stretched along the northwestern frontier of the Aztec Empire and along the southeastern frontier of the Purépecha. In direct competition for land and resources, they were each blocking the other's expansion projects.

The Purépecha-Tarascans had conquered settlements and territories only to lose them to Aztec expansion, and the same was happening to the Aztecs. From 1440 and into the 1450s, the Purépecha expanded in areas away from Aztec lands and moved east to the Pacific Coast, where they acquired Zacatula. Then they expanded into the Toluca Valley, as well as north to what is now the Mexican state of Guanajuato.

The Purépecha Empire ran their new territories on the frontier differently than how the Aztecs maintained their tributary cities. The Purépecha provided support to these outlying territories from their core – their capital of Tzintzuntzan. They sent resources to their fringe territories and received from them as well, in relatively equal exchange. In the Aztec Empire, it was more a situation of taking but not necessarily giving back. The Purépecha realized they couldn't drain their provinces and endeavored to maintain cordial relations with them.

The Purépecha encouraged the new cultures they conquered to become part of the broader Purépecha culture – to wear their style of clothing and speak their language. If the other people groups assimilated into the mainstream culture, they were considered Purépecha. It wasn't a matter of birth so much as a lifestyle. They did not draw a line between the conquerors and the conquered. Their policy was gentler than the Aztecs, who didn't bother with assimilation and ruled harshly through terror. The Purépecha enjoyed greater harmony with their provinces, while the Aztecs generated animosity and resentment.

The Aztec Empire and the Purépecha Empire fought border skirmishes and jockeyed to grab new territories before the other could get there. Yet, they also experienced periods when the strained relations were relaxed, and in these seasons of détente, they would engage in trade with one another. The trade mostly ended in the mid-1400s when the rivalry intensified.

The simmering relations between the two empires finally exploded into an all-out war from 1469 to 1478. The newly crowned Huey Tlatoani of the Aztecs was Axayacatl, grandson of Moctezuma I. His youthful military skill had won the favor of Viceroy Tlacaelel of Tenochtitlan and King Nezahualcoyotl of Texcoco. When his father died, the council of rulers and elders chose Axayacatl over his two older brothers Ahuitzotl and Tizoc, even though he was only twenty.

As was typical in the region when a new ruler assumed the throne, neighboring kingdoms would take the opportunity to challenge the inexperienced king. In 1469, the year that Axayacatl was crowned king, the Purépecha instigated new border conflicts, which initially did not turn out well for them. Axayacatl was young, but he was a ferocious and shrewd warrior.

In the next few years, Axayacatl launched a bold offensive against the Purépecha. He began to systematically recapture former outlying Aztec lands that the Purépecha had taken in the previous decade. He also started capturing new territory along the edges of the Purépecha frontier, with many bloody and protracted battles between the two empires.

Emboldened by his first nine years of initial success, Axayacatl gathered a force of 32,000 Aztec fighters and marched on the city of Taximaroa (now Hidalgo), the capital city of the Purépecha territory closest to Aztec lands. Taximaroa was prepared. Axayacatl was met by a staggering 50,000 warriors defending Taximaroa – seriously outnumbered! The two armies fought for the entire day; finally, Axayacatl had no choice but to withdraw. The Purépecha had killed at least 20,000 of his men! He'd lost almost two-thirds of his army.

One can imagine Axayacatl and his men plodding home, grieving their comrades and despondent over losing the battle. They were used to winning. What happened this time? In addition to having a much bigger military force and fighting on their own turf, the Purépecha-Tarascans had another major advantage: their knowledge of metallurgy. They had shields of copper that would easily deflect arrows and spears, while the Aztec shields were wood or woven reeds. They had long spears tipped with copper, but the Aztecs used wooden clubs and short spears.

Bronze implements used by Purépecha-Tarascans found in Tzintzuntzan archeological site[iv]

Although they won the battle, this experience prompted Tzitzipandáquare, the Purépecha ruler, to build more fortifications and military centers along the Aztec border. He brokered a deal with the Otomies and Matlatzincas, who had been evicted from their homelands by the Aztecs. They were invited to live in Purépecha territory on the border with the Aztecs in return for helping defend the Purépecha lands from the Aztecs. Of course, the Otomies and Matlatzincas were more than happy to fight against the people who had rendered them homeless.

This was the first major defeat the Aztecs had ever suffered since the Triple Alliance had formed. And it happened on Axayacatl's watch. Although he would go on to win several minor triumphs in the next couple of years, this one great loss would forever shadow his reign. Axayacatl died just three years later, barely in his thirties.

Tzitzipandáquare launched a counterattack on the Aztecs later that year, reaching fifty miles out of Tenochtitlan before he was forced back. This prompted the Aztecs to work out a deal with the Purépecha for a demilitarized zone on the frontier between Aztec lands and Purépecha-Tarascan lands. This area between the Balsas and Lerma rivers was protected by strategic fortifications overlooking the valleys. Once this cease-fire was settled, the Purépecha turned their attention elsewhere, to other lands they could conquer.

When the Aztec emperor Axayacatl died, he was succeeded by his brother Tizoc in 1481. Tizoc engaged in minor frontier clashes with the Purépecha during his reign; however, the Aztecs considered him to be a weak and inept military ruler. He died after only five years on the throne. Rumors persisted that he was poisoned by Tlacaelel in a desperate plot to end his disastrous reign.

Perhaps the greatest military ruler of the Aztec Empire, Ahuitzotl, was the brother of both Axayacatl and Tizoc – all three from the same mother. He ruled Tenochtitlan from 1486 to 1502. Besides suppressing a rebellion of the Huastec people, doubling the size of the Aztec Empire, and conquering a broad swath of Mexico's Pacific Coast as far south as Guatemala, Ahuitzotl also inflamed the struggle with the Purépecha.

Rather than direct assaults on the Purépecha, Ahuitzotl initially supported and encouraged other people to attack them. He turned to the Chontales, the Cuitlatecs, and other ethnic groups who were allies or tributary cities of the Aztec Empire, enticing them to harass the Purépecha and instigate border skirmishes, in exchange for favors from the Aztecs.

After these other groups softened the defense lines, Ahuitzotl conquered the border city of Otzo in a bloody massacre; none of the population remained – all were killed or fled the area. Ahuitzotl turned the city into an Aztec military outpost. The Purépecha responded by building fortresses close to Otzo to prevent the Aztecs from using it as a foothold. Ahuitzotl then moved further west to the Pacific Coast and conquered Guerrero.

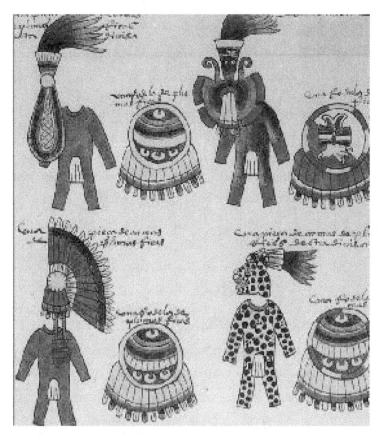

Purépecha-Tarascan traditional religious costumes.[lvi]

Beginning in 1480, the new Purépecha-Tarascan Emperor Zuangua conquered and occupied regions of what is now the Mexican states of Colima and Jalisco, gaining control of nitratine mines in the area. His reign was resisted by these people, and from 1480 to 1510, the Saltpeter War raged between the Purépecha Empire and the people of Colima, Sayula, Zapotlán, Tapalpa, and Autlán. Ultimately, the Purépecha were expelled from Colima and Jalisco.

Meanwhile, in Tenochtitlan, Ahuitzotl died, and his nephew Moctezuma II was crowned Huey Tlatoani in 1502 – the emperor who was ruling when the Spaniards arrived. Moctezuma spent the first decade of his reign consolidating the immense areas of new territory conquered by Ahuitzotl. Then, in 1515, the Aztec Empire marched against the Purépecha once again, led by the Tlaxcala general Tlahuicole. Once again, their military campaign ended in failure. Once again, the Aztec warriors withdrew in defeat.

The Purépecha Empire remained unconquered by the Aztec Empire. The Aztecs' failure to gain ascendency over the neighboring empire must have undercut their feelings of invincibility and their self-identity as a chosen people called out by Huitzilopochtli to conquer the lands around them.

The Purépecha and Aztecs soon had a common enemy, the Spanish conquistadors, who initially focused on the Aztec Empire, unaware of a second empire to the northwest. In 1520, while the Spaniards were besieging Tenochtitlan, the Purépecha emperor Zuangua died and was succeeded by Tangaxuan. Almost immediately, Tangaxuan received Aztec emissaries from Tenochtitlan, asking for the Purépecha to ally with them in their desperate struggle against the Spaniards.

Once Tangaxuan extracted crucial information from the Aztecs, he killed the emissaries. He was formulating his own plan. The Aztecs were fighting the Spaniards, and that wasn't going well. Tangaxuan formulated a different tactic, one of diplomacy. He sent a small delegation to the Spaniards to negotiate peace and received a group of the conquistadors into his kingdom, where he plied them with gold and other gifts. His plan backfired.

When Hernán Cortés saw the gold, he suddenly became interested in the Tarascan-Purépecha Empire. Once he conquered Tenochtitlan, he sent one of his captains, Cristóbal de Olid, on a military campaign against the Purépecha in 1522. Amazingly, the Purépecha did not put up a fight. They laid down their weapons. Tangaxuan persisted in his plan of a diplomatic approach rather than suffering the violent end the Aztecs had experienced.

The Tarascans submitted to the Spaniards and accepted the Catholic faith, hoping their empire could continue as a sort of tributary to the Spaniards. For the next eight years, the plan worked. Spanish friars moved in to instruct in Catholicism, while Tangaxuan continued to rule. He continued to collect tribute from his provinces, most of which he kept for himself, sending a portion on to the Spaniards. Hernán Cortés was focusing his attention elsewhere, and the Tarascans weren't causing any trouble.

Nuño de Guzmán's "conquest" of the Tarascans, who had already surrendered years earlier. Note his use of Aztec soldiers (bottom left).[lvii]

However, the arrangement all came to a sudden and violent end when Nuño de Guzmán was appointed by Spain as the first president of the newly formed *Royal Audiencia of Mexico*. When Guzmán discovered that Tangaxuan had continued as de facto ruler of the Tarascans, he charged him with withholding tribute, heresy, and sodomy, holding a trial by torture. In 1530, Tangaxuan, the last emperor of the Tarascan-Purépecha Empire, was horribly executed.

Fray Jeronimo de Acalá, in *Relación de Michoacán,* documented how Guzmán had the emperor wrapped in a mat tied it to a horse's tail; the mat was set on fire with the horse dragging it around as

Tangaxuan burned to death. A crier went with the horse, calling to the people, "Look and pay heed! Look, you lowly people who are all rogues."

This marked the end of the Tarascan-Purépecha Empire. They had coexisted in mutual respect with the Spanish missionaries for eight years, and now they saw the darker, humiliating, cruel side of their new empire, the side the Aztecs had been experiencing for the past decade.

PART THREE
THE SPANISH CONQUEST

Chapter 9: Cortés's Arrival

The year was 1518, and Moctezuma II, Aztec emperor of Tenochtitlan, was troubled. Disturbing omens were disquieting his people: a fire burning in the night sky, the waters of Lake Texcoco suddenly boiling up with high waves flooding the city, a woman wailing in the night – some said it was their mother goddess Coatlicue.

Two years earlier, King Nezahualpilli of Texcoco, his friend and Triple Alliance co-ruler, had died. Nezahualpilli, a seer, had once prophesied that foreigners would overpower the empire. Nezahualpilli's father, Nezahualcoyotl, had prophesied that the great temple would be destroyed in a *one-reed year*. In the Aztec calendar of 52 years, the next year would be a one-reed year. And now, foreigners had arrived in the Mayan region of Yucatan.

Moctezuma was concerned about the unsettled state of the Aztec Empire. After Nezahualpilli died, contention over which son would be Texcoco's next monarch exploded into civil war. Moctezuma had supported Cacamatzin, but the war had ended with the kingdom of Texcoco split three ways between three sons. Cacamatzin ruled the capital city, his brother Ixtlilxochitl – now the sworn enemy of Moctezuma – ruled the northern third of the land, and a third brother ruled the rest. Tenochtitlan and Texcoco had been powerful allies for almost a century. Could Moctezuma depend on the fractured Texcoco in what loomed ahead?

The strange foreigners had first been seen the year earlier in three peculiar and enormous boats that could each carry thirty men or more. The Mayan people had fought and killed over half of them and driven them off. Moctezuma had relaxed momentarily; these aliens were mortal and could be overcome. But this year, four more boats had come. This time they had defeated the Mayan city of Champoton, killing or driving out all the residents. And now their ships were headed north, toward Aztec territory.

Moctezuma II, Huey Tlatoani of Tenochtitlan, 1502-1520[viii]

Who were these people? Moctezuma decided to find out. He called a group of his nobles and asked them to take gifts and swiftly travel to the coast. He'd heard these foreigners were interested in gold, so he told his emissaries to include some gold with the gifts. He instructed them to gather information on these men with the shining armor.

What Moctezuma may not have known is that two of these unusual strangers had been living in the Yucatan for the past seven years, victims of shipwreck. In 1511, a small Spanish ship was sailing from Panama to Santo Domingo when it wrecked on a sandbar. Sixteen men and two women climbed into the lifeboat and were carried north by a strong current to the Yucatan Peninsula. The dozen or so who were still alive were captured by the Mayans, who immediately sacrificed the captain and four others. The rest were consigned to slavery, and all but two died of disease or being overworked.

The two survivors, a Franciscan priest named Jerónimo de Aguilar and a sailor named Gonzalo Guerrero, managed to escape. But they were later captured by a rival Mayan tribe led by Chief Xamanzana. They lived with Xamanzana's tribe, learning the language and adapting to the new culture. Guerrero proved his worth as a fighter and was rewarded by becoming a war chief; he married a woman from Mayan nobility and began a family.

Six years later, Francisco Hernández de Córdoba petitioned the governor of Cuba for permission to head an expedition to search and explore new lands and resources. At least, that's the story he told Governor Diego Velázquez de Cuéllar. More likely, based on his personal writings, he and his friends needed more indigenous people as slaves for the mines and plantations of Cuba. Permission was granted, and Córdoba set sail from Cuba in 1517 with three ships and 110 men.

They found Mexico by accident after a strong storm blew them to the coast of Yucatan. From their ships, they were amazed to see a large urban area with masonry buildings. The Europeans had not yet encountered a sophisticated culture like this in the New World. On March 4, 1517, the Mayans approached their ships in ten *pirogues* (canoes) with sails and oars. The people smiled and appeared friendly, communicating through sign language that they would come the next day with more boats to help them to land.

They did return the next day, but this time they weren't friendly. Once the Spaniards arrived on shore, the Mayans ambushed them. The Spaniards desperately fought back with their crossbows and firearms and managed to escape back to their ships. They sailed on, but they had run out of water; eventually, thirst drove them to anchor and go ashore to find water. That night, the Mayan chief Mochcouoh attacked them, killing 57 of their men and capturing two more – who were probably sacrificed.

The remainder of the men made it back to the ship, but Córdoba's body was full of arrows, and several other men were mortally wounded. Five died on the voyage back; Córdoba and three more men died just after arriving in Cuba. Sixty-eight of the original 110 perished. Despite the massive casualties, the stories the survivors told of remarkable architecture comparable to European buildings piqued the interest of Governor Velázquez of Cuba. With such an advanced civilization, he strongly suspected this new land had gold and other wealth to be exploited.

Expedition of Juan De Grijalva, 1518[ix]

Governor Velázquez wasted no time organizing another expedition. Juan de Grijalva sailed from Cuba in April 1518 with four ships and 170 men. Grijalva's orders were to get all the gold and silver he could acquire and bring it back to Velázquez. Grijalva sailed directly to Champoton, where the indigenous people had so mercilessly slaughtered Córdoba's men. Once again, the Mayans attacked, but Grijalva was prepared. This time the Spaniards won, and the Mayans fled.

Grijalva continued the voyage, sailing westward along the Yucatan peninsula, which the pilot insisted was an island. They arrived in the Tabasco region and were greeted by the local people. The Spaniards gifted them with colored glass beads, and the indigenous people reciprocated with gold necklaces and small gold figurines of lizards and birds. They told the Spaniards much gold could be found in the west.

Grijalva continued to sail along the coastline when they saw men on the beach waving white banners, signaling them to come ashore. At this point, they were in the Boca del Rio area, in the Aztec territory – and almost due east from Tenochtitlan. They dropped anchor and went ashore, where they met with the people who had been waving the flags. They were Aztecs, the men Moctezuma had sent to find out more about these strange new people. The Aztec emissaries presented Grijalva with intricately carved gold items, while the conquistadors gave them glass beads. Grijalva took one of the Aztec men with him for a translator, who was baptized and given the name Francisco.

Grijalva claimed the territory for the crown and for Governor Velázquez, giving it the name of *New Spain* (which later came to be used for all the Spanish colonies in the Americas and the Pacific islands). By this point, his navigator had finally realized they had reached another continent –not just an island. When Grijalva arrived back in Cuba and gave Velázquez the gold items and his report, the governor began organizing yet another expedition.

Hernán Cortés[k]

Several months later, on October 23, 1518, Velázquez commissioned Hernán Cortés to lead a third expedition with the objective of exploring, spreading Christianity, and exchanging items with the local people. He did *not* give permission to establish a colony. Cortés set sail to Mexico on February 10, 1519, landing first at Cozumel in the Yucatan peninsula in Mayan territory. He had 11 ships, 109 sailors, 508 soldiers, 16 horses, 13 muskets, ten heavy artillery, four light artillery, and 32 crossbows. Cortés brought two translators: Francisco, the Aztec, and Melchor, a young Mayan man Córdoba had captured earlier. A conquistador on the expedition, Bernal Díaz del Castillo, later chronicled the conquest in *Historia Verdadera de la Conquista de la Nueva España (The True History of the Conquest of New Spain).*

At Cozumel, Cortés heard about the two Spanish men living in the Yucatan since being shipwrecked eight years earlier. He sent messengers to them with ransom (more glass beads) for the Mayans. Father Jerónimo de Aguilar happily joined the conquistadors, serving as another translator, which worked out well since Melchor managed to slip away back to his own people two days later.

On the other hand, Gonzalo Guerrero had gone native with tattoos and piercings. The Spanish Inquisition was going on, and he could probably imagine being stretched on the rack and burned at the stake for abandoning his faith. When Father Aguilar tried to convince him to come with him, he replied (as recorded by Bernal Díaz del Castillo),

> "Brother Aguilar, I am married and have three children, and they look on me as a cacique (lord) here, and captain in time of war. My face is tattooed, and my ears are pierced. What would the Spaniards say about me if they saw me like this? Go, and God's blessing be with you, for you have seen how handsome these children of mine are. Please give me some of those beads you have brought to give to them, and I will tell them that my brothers have sent them from my own country."

Cortés claimed Cozumel for the Spanish crown in March 1519 before setting sail again for the Tabasco region. A year earlier, the Maya-speaking Potoncan people had been cordial with Grijalva, but this time they attacked. Cortés defeated them, captured some of their men as prisoners, and claimed Tabasco for the crown. He was far outnumbered by the Potoncan, but his men fought with guns and cannons, and they terrified the indigenous people by fighting on horseback. They had never seen horses, and they thought the horse and man were all one diabolical creature.

After another failed attack, the Potoncan chiefs approached with gold and other gifts, apologizing for their inhospitable behavior. Cortés forgave them and accepted their gifts but ordered them to stop worshiping idols, which they agreed to do. Cortés asked the Potoncan people where they got their gold, and they told him from Culchua (Cholula) in the interior.

Doña Marina, known as La Malinche[xi]

The Potoncan gave 20 women to the Spaniards, and they were baptized as Christians. One woman, Doña Marina, known as La Malinche, became Cortés's mistress and gave birth to his son Martin. She was a Nahuatl-speaking Aztec but had been given or sold to the Maya as a child and was fluent in both Nahuatl and Maya. Her knowledge of both languages made her invaluable as a translator. She didn't know Spanish yet, but Father Aguilar could ask her questions in Mayan, which she could then translate into the Aztecan Nahuatl.

On March 23, Cortés sailed to Veracruz. When he landed on Easter Sunday, he was approached by two Aztec emissaries, Tendile and Pitalpitoque. Doña Marina and Father Aguilar translated their message: they came to welcome them and learn more about them. The Aztecs built a shelter for the Spaniards, served them a meal, and gave them gifts. They then sat down to paint pictures of Cortés, Father Aguilar, a dog, and a cannon, which they took back to Tenochtitlan to show Moctezuma.

Cortés gave them a demonstration of what his large and small canon, muskets, and crossbows could do. He gave them gifts of glass beads and other items, including a soldier's helmet that he asked them to return to him filled with gold dust. Just as he requested, about a week later, over a hundred men returned, with the helmet full of gold dust along with costly treasures of intricately carved gold and silver items. They also politely relayed Moctezuma's message that Cortés was *not* invited to travel to Tenochtitlan to see the emperor.

Cortés calmly expressed how essential it was that he meet Moctezuma. He gave more gifts for them to take back to the emperor as well as personal gifts for the ambassadors. He asked them to go back to their leader and convince Moctezuma to receive Cortés and his entourage. Shortly after, the emissaries returned, with more gifts of gold but with the emperor's final answer: Cortés was not allowed to see him, and that was the end of the discussion.

For the moment, Cortés turned to other matters. Governor Diego Velázquez of Cuba had only commissioned him to explore new territory, collect treasure, and convert the indigenous people to Catholicism, *not* establish any settlements. Daringly, Cortés colonized anyway, building Villa Rica de la Vera Cruz, which he declared independent of Cuba and subject only to King Charles, the Holy Roman Emperor and monarch of Spain.

Cortés resigned his commission from Velázquez, appointed some of his men for a town council, and then accepted their nomination to be governor-general of the new colony. He immediately sent a ship to Spain with the gold they had collected, accompanied by letters to the king. They described to King Charles all they had discovered and accomplished and their rationale for declaring independence from Cuba and Governor Velázquez.

Once that was all settled, it was time to march to Tenochtitlan! Ignoring Moctezuma's injunction *not* to come, Cortés left 100 men in Veracruz under his trusted captain Juan de Escalante, then marched into the interior in mid-August 1519 with the rest of his soldiers, 15 horsemen, and 15 cannons. Father Aguilar, Doña Marina, and the Aztec Francisco (who had learned Spanish in the past year) also came along; between these three interpreters, they were able to communicate with the various people they encountered.

Cempoala, in relation to Tenochtitlan and other Aztec cities[xii]

They reached Cempoala, 25 miles inland, where they resided for two months with the Totonac people. About seventy years earlier, the Totonac people had been conquered by the Aztecs and were now a tributary city. They communicated to Cortés how they loathed their rulers, who demanded tribute payments twice a year, but even worse, they took their children for slave labor and sacrifices to Huitzilopochtli. The Totonac told Cortés they weren't the only disgruntled ones; many conquered city-states in the Aztec frontier were bitter toward Moctezuma.

Just as Cortés was developing friendly relations with the Totonac, he received word of an urgent situation back in the settlement of Villa Rica de la Vera Cruz. Some of the men he left there were loyal to Velázquez; they deplored Cortés' mutiny and how he had gone behind the governor's back to the King of Spain. They were scheming to send one of the ships to Cuba to warn Velázquez. On receiving this news, Cortés rushed back to Vera Cruz, rounded up the conspirators, and hanged the two ringleaders. He cut off the navigator's feet and whipped the rest of the men involved. He also scuttled all the ships, preventing anyone from traveling back to Cuba.

With order restored on the coast, Cortés headed back to Cempoala to resume his mission of diplomacy. With great finesse, he negotiated an alliance with the Totonacs of Cempoala; they agreed to join their warriors with his military force. While he was there, some Aztec emissaries arrived to collect the semi-annual tribute from Cempoala. Cortés cunningly persuaded the Totonac to refuse the tribute and imprison the Aztec delegates. He then freed Moctezuma's officials, feigning innocence in the matter and telling them to inform the emperor that he was willing to assist the Aztecs with the problem of rebellious cities. He skillfully instigated rebellion among the Totonac while assuring Moctezuma that he would ally with the Aztecs against the rebels.

With the Totonac warriors accompanying them, it was now time to resume the march toward Tenochtitlan. Their next challenge would be to subdue the fierce Tlaxcala, the incessant and unconquered enemies of the Aztec, and enlist them in the plan to overcome the mighty Aztec empire.

Chapter 10: The Massacre of Cholula

Tlaxcala lay ahead. What sort of welcome would the conquistadors receive? It was August of 1519, and Cortés and his men, joined by the Totonac warriors, resumed the march toward Tenochtitlan. They were approaching Tlaxcala, a loose confederacy of about 200 towns. Cortés had heard of the fierce reputation of these people but knew they were in constant war with Tenochtitlan. Would they be friendly or hostile?

The Tlaxcala people greeted the Spaniards in full battle array, ferociously fighting Cortés and his allies for three days. Despite their superior weaponry and armor, the Spaniards were succumbing to the brutal assault by the vicious warriors. Conquistador Bernal Díaz del Castillo wrote that the Spaniards were surrounded on every side and probably would have all been killed if the Tlaxcala had not had a sudden change of heart.

Whenever the Tlaxcala fought the frequent battles with the Aztecs, any warriors captured by the other side would be sacrificed to the gods. When they fought Cortés, he amazed them by what he did with the Tlaxcala he captured. The next day, he would return any prisoners-of-war, accompanied by messages of peace and reminders that he too was an enemy of the Aztecs. Eventually, the Tlaxcala realized that the Spaniards would be more useful as allies against the hated Aztecs. The elders convinced their war chief to end the fighting, and with Doña Marina and Father Aguilar translating, they negotiated a truce. Cortés stayed with the Tlaxcala for 20 days, plotting his next move.

Tlaxcala allied with Cortés; painting by unknown Aztec scribes[lxiii]

The great city-state of Cholula lay ahead, with a population of 100,000. The Olmec were believed to have settled the area around 100 BC. Later, a group of Toltecs had migrated there after the fall of Tula. Cholula had become a dominant political force in the region, a center for trade, and a destination for religious pilgrimages. The largest pyramid in all of Mesoamerica stood there, and Cortés estimated 430 temples.

For years, Cholula had existed in an informal alliance with the Tlaxcala, 20 miles to the north. However, the Aztecs exerted great pressure; just two years earlier, Cholula had capitulated and allied with the Aztecs. This meant abandoning their alliance with the Tlaxcala, mortal enemies of the Aztecs; this turned out badly for them as Cortés was now headed their way with 1000 Tlaxcala warriors.

Cortés was still debating his options: whether to start an all-out war with the Aztecs or to continue with a diplomatic approach. Since Cholula was allied with the Aztecs, he had to tread carefully. Back in Tenochtitlan, Moctezuma was fully aware of Cortés's trek toward his kingdom and ordered the Cholula to stop the Spanish. Cortés and his men marched into Cholula with no resistance. However, the city leaders did not come out to greet them, and no one offered them food or water.

Cortés's indigenous friends were uneasy. The Totonac noted fortifications being constructed. Doña Marina took the opportunity to chat with the women of the city in her native Nahuatl language. She learned that the Cholula were planning to murder the Spaniards as they were sleeping. The Tlaxcala were thirsty for revenge against the Cholula for abandoning their alliance, and they kept pushing Cortés to launch an attack.

Finally, Cortés strode into the main temple and confronted the rulers of the city. Yes, they admitted, Moctezuma had ordered them to resist the Spaniards, but they hadn't followed through with his orders. Cortés considered what they were saying, and then he considered the battle preparations his allies had noticed and what Doña Marina had heard. Deciding he could not trust the people of Cholula, he gave the command for a preemptive strike.

The Spaniards and their indigenous allies rounded up the nobility and massacred them, killing 3000 people in three hours. They then set fire to the great, ancient city. This mass killing of a people who had not (yet) been aggressive sent shock waves through the Aztec Empire. Many cities considered it wise to align with the conquistadors rather than risk annihilation. It was at this point that Moctezuma gave in and invited Cortés to visit his city of Tenochtitlan.

The great day arrived. On November 8, 1519, ten months after sailing from Cuba, Cortés and his amassed forces marched unhindered over the causeway that led to Tenochtitlan. He had never seen a city this size. With an estimated population of 200,000, Tenochtitlan probably outnumbered most cities in Europe. An island city in Lake Texcoco, Tenochtitlan had a system of causeways connecting it to points on the mainland and a nearby island.

Moctezuma greets Cortés.[lxiv]

On his litter decorated with feathers, Moctezuma was carried out on the causeway to meet Cortés, with his younger brother Cuitlahuac, his nephew Cacamatzin (co-regent of Texcoco, Tenochtitlan's ally), and his elders and war chiefs. The Aztec rulers were magnificently adorned with feathers, jewels, and gold. The people of the city stood along the causeway and in the high buildings of Tenochtitlan, watching the encounter. Moctezuma formally welcomed Cortés, who introduced himself as the representative of Queen Juana and her son, King Charles of Spain and Holy Roman Emperor.

An awkward moment ensued when Cortés attempted to greet Moctezuma with a customary Castilian embrace, quickly intercepted by Cuitlahuac and Cacamatzin, who made it clear that touching the emperor just wasn't done. Moctezuma eased Cortés's embarrassment by placing a chain of gold around his neck, followed by a garland of flowers. He then led Cortés to the shrine of the goddess Toci, where, according to the *Florentine Codex*, he said:

> "My lord . . . you have come to your city; you have come to sit on your place, on your throne. Oh, it has been reserved to you for a small time, it was conserved by those who have gone, your substitutes . . .This is what has been told by our rulers . . .that you would come to ask for your throne, your place, that you would come here. Come to the land, come and rest; take possession of your royal houses, give food to your body."

If Moctezuma really said this, he was acknowledging that Cortés was Quetzalcoatl, coming back in the year one reed, as Quetzalcoatl had said he would. If Moctezuma believed this, why did he resist Cortés all those months?

Moctezuma housed Cortés and his chief officers in the royal palace of his deceased father, Axayacatl. According to Bernal Díaz del Castillo, the emperor accepted Cortés as representative of the king of Spain, pledging his loyalty and saying, "As for your great King, I am in his debt and will give him of what I possess." Díaz said that in the palace, the Spaniards found the secret treasure room with golden plates and jewels. "The sight of all that wealth dumbfounded me."

Moctezuma's friendliness deteriorated when Cortés wanted to place a cross and an image of the Virgin Mary in the Templo Major, at the top of the grand pyramid. The emperor and his elders were infuriated, saying they could not offend their gods who gave them health, rain, crops, and victories in battle.

Six days after his arrival in Tenochtitlan, Cortés received the news of an attack on his new town of Villa Rica de la Vera Cruz, 200 miles away on the coast. Qualpopoca, Moctezuma's military commander, had led a force of Aztecs, killing Cortés's dear friend Juan de Escalante, who Cortés had left in charge of the settlement, along with six other Spaniards and many Totonacs.

In response to this treachery, Cortés, accompanied by Doña Marina, Father Aguilar, and five of his captains, accosted Moctezuma, ordering him to come quietly with them to their quarters in Axayacatl's palace. "Don't cry out! Don't raise a commotion! If you do, we will kill you immediately!" From that time on, Moctezuma lived under house arrest with Cortés in Axayacatl's palace.

Moctezuma continues to reign under house arrest.[xv]

Despite his imprisonment, Moctezuma continued to oversee affairs of the empire, but under the control of Cortés. Moctezuma assured his people that he had willingly moved into Cortés's palace under the instructions of the gods. The Aztecs were doubtful; they also were growing increasingly perturbed by the presence of the 1000 Tlaxcala warriors in their city, their hated enemies, but allies of Cortés.

With Moctezuma in house arrest, Cortés sent his men to investigate sources of gold in the provinces and forced Moctezuma to pay tribute to the Spanish crown. The Spaniards melted down the gold figurines in the palace and formed gold bars. Cortés also built a Catholic altar in the Templo Major but left the Aztec idols.

The Aztecs were growing increasingly agitated; their priests were saying their gods were angry and would all leave unless the Aztecs killed the Spaniards or forced them back across the sea. Moctezuma warned the Spaniards that they were in mortal danger. With their emperor detained, most of the nobility were turning to his brother Cuitlahuac for leadership. But they hesitated to act without a direct order from Moctezuma. This unsettled state of affairs continued for five months.

Then, in April 1520, Moctezuma alerted Cortés that his men had observed a fleet of 19 Spanish ships with 1400 soldiers landing on the coast. Under the command of Pánfilo de Narváez, the troops had been sent by Velázquez, Governor of Cuba, to arrest or kill Cortés for defying the governor's orders. On hearing this news, Cortés left some of his soldiers in Tenochtitlan under the command of Pedro de Alvarado, a seasoned conquistador, giving him strict instructions not to allow Moctezuma to escape.

Cortés and the rest of his troops marched quickly to Cempoala, where Narváez had set up camp. With a surprise night attack, Cortés captured Narváez and convinced the rest of the Spanish soldiers to come over to his side. He told them of the gold they had acquired and promised to make them all rich. With his new recruits, Cortés marched back to Tenochtitlan with 1300 soldiers, 96 horses, and 2000 Tlaxcala warriors.

Cortés was horrified to return to a chaotic situation in Tenochtitlan. In his absence, Alvarado and his fellow conquistadors had killed hundreds of unarmed Aztec nobles in an unprovoked attack, which became known as the *Massacre in the Great Temple*. Cortés interrogated Alvarado and his men and also questioned the Aztecs to try to piece together what had happened on May 22, 1520.

Pedro de Alvarado.[lxvi]

While Cortés was gone, Moctezuma had requested permission to celebrate the important festival of Toxcatl, which honored Tezcatlipoca, a chief Aztec god (you might remember him as the god who tricked Quetzalcoatl, leading to his downfall). Alvarado gave permission, with the stipulation of no human sacrifices and that none of the participants could carry weapons. Normally, a young man who had been impersonating Tezcatlipoca through the past year was sacrificed at this festival, but apparently, the Aztecs decided to follow Alvarado's orders.

About 1000 Aztec noblemen had gathered in the grounds surrounding the great temple, naked but draped in jewels, gold, and silver and wearing elaborate feather headdresses. Drums beat loudly, accompanied by the shrill sound of wind instruments. The men danced in circles, holding hands, singing along with the musicians, praising Tezcatlipoca, and asking him to provide water, grain, good health, and victory. Everyone was enjoying the festival, dancing, and singing, with the music roaring like waves.

Suddenly, Alvarado and the Spanish soldiers appeared, blocking all the exits with ten or twelve men. They then turned on the musicians and dancers, rushing toward the man playing the drums and cutting off both his arms and then his head with such force that it sailed through the air. With no remorse or pity, they brutally slew the celebrants, stripping off their gold and jewels. They sliced off heads and arms, stabbed the men in the gut, so their entrails flowed out, and dashed some to the ground, so their heads were crushed.

The Aztecs ran to the exits but were met and killed by the laughing Spaniards guarding the way out. Some lay down, pretending to be dead, as the blood of the dead ran like water over them, and the stench of entrails filled the air. Others climbed over the walls and screamed to those outside, "Come quickly! Come with spears and shields! Our warriors have been murdered! They have been annihilated!" The Mexica quickly stormed the temple with spears, bows, and javelins. They furiously hurled a barrage of yellow javelins at the Spaniards.

Different explanations were given for the motivation of the massacre. Alvarado told Cortés he had received information that the Aztecs were planning to attack the Spaniards during the festival, so the slaughter was a preemptive strike. Some said they intervened to prevent a human sacrifice, although most of the Spaniards said the Aztecs were only singing and dancing. The Aztecs felt that the Spaniards had attacked the noblemen to steal their gold and jewels.

By the time Cortés got back to Tenochtitlan, the Aztecs had blockaded the palace where the Spaniards were staying and where Moctezuma was still being held. They had elected Cuitlahuac, Moctezuma's brother, as their new tlatoani, renouncing Moctezuma. Somehow, in the confusion and chaos, Moctezuma was killed – a mysterious death.

Moctezuma II struck by stones.[lvii]

In the Spanish account, Cortés desperately tried to restore order by commanding Moctezuma to come out to the balcony of the palace and speak to the people, asking them to allow the Spaniards to leave the city peacefully and return to the coast. The people scorned his words and threw rocks and darts at him, which the Spaniards tried to deflect with their shields. Diaz reported that three rocks hit Moctezuma, one on the head. He refused treatment and died three days later. The Aztecs said that Moctezuma was strangled by the Spaniards. At this point, the renounced emperor no longer served a purpose for either side.

The Spaniards and their indigenous allies were in a perilous state, running out of water, food, and gunpowder. Cortés requested a one-week ceasefire from the Aztecs, promising that the Spaniards would return all the treasures they had stolen and would leave the city peacefully. Instead of waiting a week, the Spaniards attempted to slip out of the city that night.

Tenochtitlan had multiple causeways running from the island to the mainland or adjoining islands. Each causeway had several gaps covered by bridges that would be removed at night. The Spaniards constructed a portable bridge to take with them, so they could cross those spans. They packed up the gold and other treasures they had accumulated and allowed the Spanish soldiers to take what they wanted. Many of the soldiers filled their pockets and were draped with heavy gold and jewels.

On July 1, 1520, Cortés and his men slipped out of the palace at night, heading for the Tlacopan causeway. A rainstorm aided their escape, blurring visibility and keeping most people indoors. They made it to the causeway and placed their portable bridge over the first gap, but suddenly an alarm went up in the city. A woman drawing water had seen them, as had a priest standing on top of the great pyramid. They hurried across the first span on the portable bridge, but the men had difficulty pulling it back up.

Suddenly, they were attacked from behind and from hundreds of canoes in the water. The Spaniards rushed as fast as possible across the causeway, but they were hindered by the great chests of treasure they were carrying. Some of the soldiers who were weighed down by the heavy gold and jewels in their pockets and belts and around their necks lost their balance and fell into the water, where they drowned.

La Noche Triste, the Night of Weeping.[lxviii]

Cortés and his chief officers were on horseback and had leaped over the open spans of the causeway. But the infantry on foot were desperately fighting the Aztec hordes while attempting to cross the spans. Much of the gold and jewels they had carried out of the city was dropped on the road or fell into the water. Unaware of their plight, Cortés and his horsemen had charged ahead and reached the mainland.

When Cortés turned around, he realized the wretched situation his men were in, as he watched wounded and bloodied Spaniards and Tlaxcala limping in. He turned and rode back out on the causeway, weeping as he realized the extent of the slaughter. Cortés himself was wounded, all the artillery was lost. As many as 1000 Spaniards were killed and at least 2000 of their indigenous allies. Some of the Aztec royals who were supportive of the Spaniards also died: Montezuma's son Chimalpopoca, the Tepanec prince Tlaltecatzin, and King Cacamatzin of Texcoco with his three sisters and two brothers. This dark, rainy night of horror was remembered as *La Noche Triste,* the night of weeping.

Chapter 11: The Fall of Tenochtitlan

With the Aztecs in hot pursuit, the Tlaxcala guided the Spaniards around Lake Zumpango, north of Lake Texcoco. Three-quarters of the Spanish conquistadors had perished, and most of the remaining survivors were wounded. Cortés had suffered a head wound but gave orders to press on to a safer place. He later recorded these events in his letters to King Charles, the *Cartas y Relaciones de Hernan Cortés al Emperador Carlos V.*

Guided by their allies, the Spaniards stumbled toward the safety of Tlaxcala lands, carrying their wounded on their backs or on the horses. They constantly fended off skirmishes from bands of Aztecs, who killed one of their horses; starving, they ate the animal, not even leaving his skin. After several days, exhausted and suffering from their wounds, they made it to the town of Otumba, about 50 miles from Tenochtitlan.

The Aztecs swarmed on them in Otumba with such a violent attack that they thought their last day had come. Bernal Díaz del Castillo wrote that the Castilian calvary brought victory in the desperate battle. Time after time, the Spaniards on horseback broke through the Aztec ranks, striking them down right and left.

The Aztecs had never experienced a calvary charge. Even so, an estimated horde of 40,000 Aztecs threatened to overwhelm the Spaniards.

Battle of Otumba, by Manuel Rodriguez de Guzman.[lix]

Cortés's battle strategy also helped win the day. He instructed the troops to focus on the Aztec leaders and captains. Recognizing an Aztec war chief from his distinctive armor and headdress, Cortés's men separated the warriors from their chief, while a conquistador slew the chief and delivered his battle-standard to Cortés. With their leader dead, the Aztecs faltered, and the Tlaxcala and Spaniards were able to rout them. The war of Otumba was won, but all the 440 surviving conquistadors and countless Tlaxcala were wounded.

The weary victors stood on the hill near Otumba, looking at the mountains in the distance, which their allies told them was Tlaxcala land, where they would find safety and rest. Finally, one week after leaving Tenochtitlan, they reached safety in the town of Gualipan. The people received them with kindness, tending their wounds and providing food and water.

Cortés and his army remained there for three days, meeting with the Tlaxcala nobles from around the region. They promised Cortés they would fight to the death with him against their enemies, as they already had proved they would. In return, they asked for the city of Cholula, an equal share of the plunder, and exemption from future tribute. Once the alliance was renewed, the Tlaxcala told the Spaniards to consider themselves at home and to rest and recover.

For the next few months, the Spaniards rested and recouped, preparing for their next assault. Everything may have seemed bleak for the Spaniards after *La Noche Triste*, but Cortés was determined to defy all odds to reach his goal of conquering the Aztec empire. Reinforcements came from the Villa Rica de la Vera Cruz settlement on the coast, along with the fortuitous arrival of supply ships from Cuba (intended for Narváez) and Spain, bringing more men and horses.

During this time, Cortés formed alliances with the cities of the Acolhua people on the eastern shores of Lake Texcoco. King Ixtlilxochitl, one of the three vice-regents of Texcoco and an enemy of Moctezuma II, sent emissaries to Cortés, offering his troops in the siege of Tenochtitlan. In return, he asked assistance in overcoming the other two vice-regents of Texcoco. These alliances were indispensable for allowing access to Lake Texcoco, not to mention providing more warriors and laborers. One by one, the allied forces worked their way along both sides of the lake and to the east, negotiating treaties with cities, including Huexotzinco, Chalco, Tlamanalco, Xochimilco, Otomi, and Tepanec.

Meanwhile, in September 1520, the Aztecs were struck with smallpox, lasting almost three months. This diminished their population and kept their attention off attacking the Spaniards or defending their city-states around the lake. Among those who died was Cuitlahuac, Moctezuma's brother and the new emperor. He was succeeded by his cousin Cuauhtémoc, the last Aztec emperor.

In the spring, the Aztecs rallied enough to launch four attacks on the Spaniards and lost each time.

Since Tenochtitlan was an island city, and the causeways had proved a major complication, Cortés hit on the ingenious idea of building a fleet of 13 small and shallow brigantines for navigating around Lake Texcoco. He set his master carpenter/boat builder Martin Lopez to work, using rigging, hardware, and sails salvaged from the scuttled boats. His master plan was to carry the disassembled brigantines overland and put them together near the lake.

Brigantine.[lx]

While his men and allies went to work cutting lumber and building the small ships, Cortés set out on a scouting mission around Lake Texcoco and the adjoining lakes. After surveying the land and taking note of how best to invade Tenochtitlan by land and water, Cortés built a 12-foot-deep canal on the eastern side of the lake extending toward where they were building the brigantines. They still had to lug all the pieces of the ships for over a mile. It took 50 days and 8000 people to build the parts of the ships, haul them to the canal, assemble, and then launch them, using labor from the people of Texcoco.

The ships were launched in the canal with sails and oars and cannons on April 28, 1521. Cortés reviewed his Spanish troops, counting 86 horses with riders, 118 archers and musketeers, over 700-foot soldiers with swords and shields, three heavy iron cannons, and fifteen small copper cannons. Each brigantine held 25 men: 12 rowers, 12 crossbow archers and musketeers, and a captain. He rallied the troops by telling them to take fresh courage and renewed spirits since God was leading them to victory, which should inspire them with courage and zeal to conquer or die.

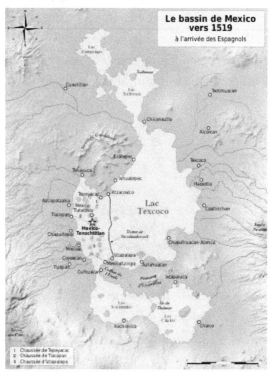

Lake Texcoco with adjoining lakes and nearby territories in as it appeared in 1519. Tenochtitlan is on the western shore connected by causeways to the mainland.[lxxi]

The joint forces of 20,000 indigenous warriors allied with Cortés's men and ships, horses, and cannons sent shock waves across the lake. One division headed to the island of Chapultepec to cut off the aqueduct that provided fresh water to Tenochtitlan. The ships and other two land forces targeted the city of Iztapalapa, just across the causeway from Tenochtitlan, giving them a chance to try out the brigantines. They were able to surround the city and score what Cortés called "a most brilliant victory."

As the brigantines approached Iztapalapa, some people had run up the mountain next to the city and sent smoke signals, alerting Tenochtitlan. Suddenly, an immense fleet of about 500 canoes charged toward Iztapalapa. When they got close to the ships, they suddenly stopped and floated silently, perhaps wondering how the ships got into the lake and what they were able to do.

In a few minutes, a wind arose, blowing from behind the ships. Cortés instantly gave orders to his commanders to sail toward the canoes, breaking through them and pursuing them. The Aztecs fled as fast as they could paddle, but the wind pushed the brigantines, and they bore down through the midst of the canoes, breaking them and throwing the Aztecs into the water. They followed the canoes for three leagues until those who were left took refuge in the city of Tenochtitlan.

A division of Cortés's army led by Pedro de Alvarado was posted on the hills of Coyoacan, just south of Tenochtitlan, watching and cheering when they saw how well the 13 brigantines performed and how fast they cut through the water. Alvarado's men had just severed the aqueduct carrying fresh water to Tenochtitlan, as thermal springs around the city made the water brackish. Now, this contingent headed for the island city.

A great battle began on the causeway, but this time the Spaniards had the advantage. The brigantines surrounding the city hindered the Aztecs from defending the causeway with their canoes. When Aztecs from other cities around the lake launched a rear attack from the mainland, Cortés ordered some of the calvary to guard the causeway and 10,000 indigenous allies to guard the shore along the lake opposite of Tenochtitlan. At this point, Alvarado's division arrived, fending off the Aztecs who had launched the rear attack and cutting through the causeways to the city. This allowed the brigantines to access the water all around the city and also cut land access to the city, making it difficult for food and reinforcements to get into the city.

Siege of Tenochtitlan, showing battles on the causeways and in the water with the brigantines and Aztec canoes. The city is not to scale; it was far larger than in this painting.[lxxii]

The Spaniards had control of the causeway with their thousands of allies from Tlaxcala and other city-states. They attempted to enter the city, but the Mexica were positioned on the rooftops, shooting arrows at anyone who neared the perimeter. Cortés decided to burn down the houses so that the Mexica wouldn't have the rooftop advantage. Using the brigantines, they burned down many houses and towers around the edge of the city.

Tenochtitlan had a network of canals, like Venice, and the brigantines sailed right into the city through the canals, using their cannons to demolish houses and other buildings. Cortés and his forces fought their way into the middle of the city, setting fire to the temples of the Templo Major religious center. Finally, after a long day of fighting, it began to get dark, so Cortés assembled his forces to return to camp.

As they were retreating, throngs of Mexica pursued them furiously, attacking their rearguard. The cavalry charged the Mexica, impaling them with their lances. Still, with howls and screams, they continued coming, raging in dismay to see their former Aztec allies

– the Texcoco, Chalca, and Otomi – burning their city and fighting against them, taunting the Mexica by calling out the names of their provinces.

In their counterattack, the Aztecs killed about 40 Spaniards and over 1000 indigenous allies. They captured some of the Spaniards alive and dragged them to the top of the tall towers in the city center, cutting open their chests and pulling out their beating hearts to offer to their gods. The Spaniards watched in horror from the perimeter.

Cortés's initial plan was to retreat to their camp on the mainland at night and make forays into the city during the day, gradually taking ground. This proved problematic, as once they left the city at night, the Aztecs would construct barricades and cover the causeways with rocks and stones to block the horses. Cortés then set up camp on the causeways, ready to fight if the Aztecs ventured out. Each morning, the Spanish forces would invade the city, gradually gaining ground.

Unable to get through the causeways, the Aztecs outside the city began smuggling in food via canoe until Cortés ordered two of the brigantines to stand guard at night. The people inside the city were running out of food and clean water. In desperation, they began drinking the brackish water in the polluted canals, which gave them dysentery. Thousands were dying from hunger, thirst, and illness.

Several more Aztec cities along the lakeshore surrendered, including Iztapalapa, Churubusco, Coluacan, and Mixquic. One month into the siege, over 20,000 of the indigenous allies returned home, frightened by a prophecy from the Aztec shamans that the Spaniards would be dead in ten days. Only about 200 of the Texcoco noblemen remained loyal through this time. Twelve days later, realizing the prophecy was false, the warriors from Tlaxcala, Cholula, Tepanec, and other tribes returned.

Forty-five days had now passed since the Spaniards first launched their brigantines and laid siege to Tenochtitlan. Cortés resolved that they needed to press harder, leveling the city to the ground, neighborhood by neighborhood, until no place was left for the Mexica to hide. On that day, he mustered over 150,000 warriors and accomplished the destruction of much of the city.

Conquistadors and indigenous allies.[lxxiii]

Cortés next ordered all three divisions to invade the city from three different points, working their way toward the marketplace in the center. Alvarado's division got there first, stopping to ascend the pyramid, set fire to Huitzilopochtli's temple, and plant the Spanish flags. Four days later, the other two divisions, led by Cortés and Sandoval, fought their way to the center.

Cortés climbed to the top of the highest tower in the Templo Major complex. From there, he realized that about seven-eighths of the city had fallen, and the rest of the population was squeezed into the remaining area. The people were starving, eating the roots and bark of the trees. Distraught, Cortés ordered his troops to stop fighting, offering terms of peace. But the Aztecs declared they would never surrender and would die fighting.

The next day they reentered the city to find the streets full of women and children, dying of hunger and sickness. Cortés ordered his men not to harm them. The Aztec men remained sequestered in their holdout and did not fight that day.

The following morning, the Spaniards and their allies assembled at daybreak, with the brigantines floating in the water just offshore from the section where the Aztecs were sequestered. When they heard a musket shot, the land troops were to invade that last holdout, driving the Aztecs toward the water and the brigantines. Everyone was told to keep a lookout for Emperor Cuauhtémoc; if they could capture him alive, the war would be over.

At that moment, a multitude of men, women, and children flooded out of the remaining buildings, stumbling and barely alive, surrendering and seeking refuge with the Spaniards. Cortés wrote that he was unable to hold back the Tlaxcala from attacking the defenseless and suffering people. Cortés wrote to King Charles,

> "We had more trouble in preventing our allies from killing with such cruelty than we had in fighting the enemy. For no race, however savage, has ever practiced such fierce and unnatural cruelty as the natives of these parts . . . I also charged the captains of our allies to forbid, by all means in their power, the slaughter of these fugitives; yet all my precautions were insufficient to prevent it, and that day more than 15,000 lost their lives."

As the Tlaxcala were brutally massacring the population, hundreds of canoes poured into the lake out of the remaining section of city. The brigantines broke into the midst of the canoes, and the captain of one ship noticed several canoes with people in regal dress. It was Emperor Cuauhtémoc, accompanied by family! He was instantly seized and delivered to Cortés.

The war was over with the capture of the emperor on August 13, 1521 – after a siege of over three months. Cuauhtémoc walked up and laid his hand on Cortés's dagger, telling Cortés to strike him to the heart. Cortés told him, "You have defended your capital like a brave warrior. A Spaniard knows how to respect valor, even in an enemy."

For the next three days, even after the surrender, the Tlaxcala looted the city, raped the women, and slaughtered the civilians, not even sparing the children. The citizens who were able to escape were permitted to settle in Tlatelolco. When the Spaniards did not find the gold and other loot they were expecting, they tortured Cuauhtémoc, broiling the soles of his feet over red-hot coals until he confessed to dumping his gold and jewels into the lake.

Torture of Cuauhtémoc. By Leandro Izaguirre[lxxiv]

Cuauhtémoc, baptized as Fernando Cuauhtémotzín, settled in Tlatelolco for four years, keeping the nominal title of tlatoani, although no longer the sovereign ruler of the empire. Then, in 1525, Cortés took Cuauhtémoc and several of his nobles with him on an expedition to Honduras, fearing that Cuauhtémoc would revolt while he was gone. On the expedition, Cortés executed the last Aztec emperor by hanging, charging his alleged conspiracy to murder Cortés and his crew.

Chapter 12: The Founding of New Spain

The Spaniards who conquered the Aztec Empire were primarily interested in three things: God, glory, and gold. Perhaps that order should be reversed. They *said* their chief objective was winning the indigenous people to the Catholic faith, but their actions (like abject cruelty and sexual exploitation of indigenous women) sent mixed messages.

Having just won their country back from Islamic rule, the church in Spain was reasserting itself as the bulwark of Catholicism. The rulers of Spain were adamant that the Catholic faith be spread in their new colonies. Consequently, Catholic friars usually accompanied the conquistadors on military campaigns, ministering to the soldiers and setting up missions for the local people as soon as an area was conquered.

The conquistadors' desire for glory and gold, along with their distance from Spain, engendered an independent and sometimes insubordinate mindset, as when Cortés defied the orders of the governor of Cuba. As New Spain rose from the ashes of the Aztec Empire, the Spanish monarchy realized they needed to rein in the conquistadors and establish a system of checks and balances. This led to the *Council of the Indies*, followed by the *Real Audiencia de México and* the *Viceroyalty of New Spain.*

King Charles of Spain established the *Council of the Indies* in 1524 as a governing body with supreme authority over all of Spain's colonies in the Americas and the Pacific islands. Four years later, he created the first *Audiencia* (high court) of Mexico to bring Cortés under the oversight and control of the monarchy. It was headed by Nuño Beltrán de Guzmán, who ruthlessly tortured and executed the Tarascan Emperor Tangaxuan, even though he had peacefully surrendered to Spain. Rather than asserting royal authority over the conquistadors, Guzmán abused his position to build his own wealth and power. In 1530 the Audiencia was dissolved, and eventually, Guzmán was arrested for treason and atrocities against the indigenous people and sent to Spain in shackles.

Viceroy don Antonio de Mendoza and Tlaxcala Indians battle with the Caxcanes in the Mixtón war, 1541-42 in Nueva Galicia.[lxxv]

King Charles appointed Don Antonio de Mendoza as the first Viceroy of New Spain (the king's *living image* in Mexico). Mendoza arrived in Mexico in 1537 to exercise authority on behalf of the king, deftly yet diplomatically curbing the power and ambition of Cortés and other conquistadors. He successfully stabilized the flare-ups between the conquistadors and the indigenous people and helped found the first two universities in Mexico: the College at Santa Cruz and the Royal and Pontifical University of Mexico.

For the most part, the leaders of New Spain maintained the preexisting internal structure of the Aztec Empire. Under Spanish rule, these city-states largely continued with either their own indigenous nobility or Spanish governors, paying tribute to the Spanish crown and continuing with their previous landholding and economic structure.

The Spanish crown rewarded the conquistadors with grants of entire indigenous communities in the *Encomienda* system of labor. The indigenous people were not slaves, per se, but working in their community as they previously had in the *calpolli* towns of Mesoamerican civilizations. In this system, each calpolli had a *tecutli* (landlord) governing the region and distributing land to the commoners. The farmers worked their designated land, and farmers and tradespeople would pay tribute to their landlord with a portion of their crops or their manufactured goods. The Encomienda system built on the pre-existing system, except now the tecutli was a Spanish lord. Some of these lords gained notoriety for the horrific abuse of their laborers.

The Aztecs had a system for slavery that included conquered people or captives from war campaigns (those who didn't get sacrificed, enslaving men, women, and children – and branding them on the cheek. Cortés owned a few hundred slaves who worked the gold mines. Slavery of the indigenous people of Mexico ended in the mid-1500s, replaced by black slaves from Africa.

When establishing the new colony of Mexico, Spain didn't send over shiploads of families to colonize the land. It was often just the conquistadors and the missionary friars, especially in the early years. The colonies in Mesoamerica comprised indigenous people with a few Spanish leaders and Catholic friars. The Franciscan (and later Dominican, Augustine, and Jesuit) friars set up missions in existing and new communities of indigenous people.

The Spaniards developed unused land areas into large cattle *ranchos* and plantations (*haciendas*), growing cash crops like banana, cotton, and coffee. These small agricultural communities often grew into towns and cities, such as Veracruz and Guadalajara. The colonists also built new Spanish cities over former great cities of the Aztecs and other indigenous people. For instance, today's sprawling Mexico City sits right on top of what was once Tenochtitlan.

Remains of the Templo Mayor of Tenochtitlan surrounded by modern Mexico City.[lxxvi]

When the Aztec Empire was replaced by New Spain, the everyday life of the indigenous people changed significantly in some areas, while other aspects of their culture continued as before. Most continued to speak Nahuatl, which had been the common language of the empire. A few of the indigenous nobility learned Spanish to communicate with the Spaniards. Spanish was mostly used for administrative affairs in the early colonial settlements.

The Spanish friars believed that the people would be more receptive to the Christian faith if it were taught in their own language. To make that happen, the friars first learned Nahuatl (and other languages) and then set about devising written Nahuatl with the Latin alphabet (the same alphabet used in Spanish, English, and most European languages). They then taught some of the indigenous boys and young men to read the Nahuatl language, so they could learn basic Christian teachings and read the parts of the Bible the friars were translating.

Santiago Mission in Jalpan, built in 16th century in Sierra Gorda, Querétaro, Mexico[lxxvii]

At first, few people of the former Aztec Empire learned Spanish. For one thing, most of the common people had no schools, so there was no venue for teaching a new language. The Spanish colonies even allowed documents, like wedding and birth certificates and title deeds, to be written in Nahuatl. It wasn't until 1714 that King Philip V of Spain ordered everyone in the Mexican colony to learn Spanish. In 1770, King Charles III mandated Spanish as the only authorized language for education, administration, and documentation (no more birth certificates in Nahuatl).

Franciscan friars learned the indigenous languages and spent much time studying the culture of the people. Through understanding the people's worldview, the friars felt they could contextualize the Gospel, presenting it in a culturally relevant way. They would transcribe their interviews with the indigenous people on their history and culture for hours on end. Some of these accounts have survived, providing us with a wealth of information on the Aztecs and other indigenous cultures in the pre-Columbian period.

Dominican friars began arriving in 1525 but questioned the efforts of the Franciscans in working within the culture of the local people. The Franciscans tended to believe that all cultures are a mixture of good and evil and that one can retain the good aspects and connect those to the teaching of faith. They didn't try to overturn the people's cultures; they just tried to root out the bad parts (like human sacrifice).

Many Dominicans believed that the pagan cultures were inherently evil – even their languages were evil; their approach was to convert the people and learn Spanish and an entirely new way of life. Priceless pre-Columbian artifacts and native codices (manuscripts) were destroyed in this quest to root out the old culture. When the people hesitated, the Dominicans complained before the Council of the Indies that the indigenous people were incapable of learning, rejected all forms of progress, and were worthy only of slavery.

Franciscan Friar Jacobo de Testera and others in his order rose to the defense of the Aztec tribes, pointing out that if they were incapable of learning, they could not have developed the sophisticated Aztec culture, with huge cities, breath-taking architecture, and exquisite craftsmanship. The first ecclesiastical council of New Spain agreed the indigenous people could understand and embrace the faith and were rational beings capable of self-government.

Most friars working on converting the Mexica and other peoples were initially pleased to see how quickly the people agreed to receive baptism into the Catholic faith. They later discovered that they had simply added Jesus and the Virgin Mary to their pantheon of gods. In the polytheistic Mesoamerican mind, these were nothing more than additional deities. For the past hundred years, the Aztecs permitted the people they conquered to continue worshiping all their other gods if they added Huitzilopochtli as their *primary god.* They didn't perceive the need to discard their gods. Syncretism (blending two or more religions) haunted the church's efforts through the centuries, and to this very day, many people groups in Mexico practice both Catholicism and their ancient religions.

The friars were divided on whether they should baptize the people first and then teach them the faith, or only baptize people who had been taught the faith and understood and received it as their own. Catholic doctrine teaches that the Holy Spirit indwells a person at their baptism (usually as infants) and initiates faith. Many friars believed that without baptizing the people first, they couldn't comprehend the teaching of faith. Thus, mass baptisms (sometimes thousands at a time) were conducted for people who had no clue of anything regarding Christianity.

Franciscan Fray Bernardino de Sahagún.[lxxviii]

Regardless of when baptism took place, the friars from all the orders agreed that the people needed to be taught the basics of the Christian faith. Fray Alonso de Molina translated the *Doctrina Christiana* (*Christian Doctrine*) in 1546, compiled a Spanish-Nahuatl confessional in 1569, and a dictionary in 1571. Franciscan Fray Bernardino de Sahagún translated a catechism, the Psalms, and the Gospels into Nahuatl, and wrote the *Florentine Codex*, which presented the history and culture of the Aztecs.

Missionary-friars went about systematically building missions throughout the country. They would have a church building for worship, an educational section for teaching basics of the faith, and living quarters for the friars. The missions also served as community centers, with shops and wineries selling products the friars produced from their farming and industry. The friars also sometimes served as government officials for their area and often were staunch defenders of basic human rights for the indigenous people, although some were guilty of abuse.

Education took a downward spiral following Spanish colonization. The Aztecs were one of the few ancient civilizations with mandatory education for both boys and girls. At age 14, boys would begin attending a *calmecac* (school for nobility) or a *telpochcalli* (school for common people). The calmecac trained teens to be administrators, priests, teachers, healers, or codex painters; subjects included history, religious rituals, reading and writing, the Aztec ideographic writing, the calendar system, astronomy, statesmanship, and theology. The commoner's school (telpochcalli) taught military fighting, history, and religion – along with a skill or trade like agriculture, craftwork, metalworking, or pottery. Teenage girls learned religious rituals, dancing, singing, household skills, and craftwork. Some girls were trained in midwifery and healing.

At first, nothing was done in the Spanish colonies for educating children, aside from some religious training. In 1536, the Franciscans collaborated with Viceroy Don Antonio de Mendoza to establish the Colegio de Santa Cruz de Tlatelolco to train indigenous young men in the priesthood. This was the first institution of higher education in the Mexico of New Spain. Boys were chosen from the former ruling families of the Aztec empire and taught Spanish, Latin, Nahuatl (reading), music, logic, philosophy, and medicine.

The college failed to produce indigenous priests, partly because the Dominicans pushed through legislation forbidding the native population from ordination to the priesthood. It did, however, produce young men with advanced language skills who provided huge aid to the Franciscans in their evangelization efforts and in recording indigenous history and culture.

The school of San José de los Naturales was founded by the Franciscans in Mexico City to train boys in trades and crafts. The Franciscans also trained scribes in the Nahuatl language to create documents such as wills, petitions to the crown, bills of sale, censuses, and other local legal records. Aside from these efforts, most of the population was unschooled and illiterate. Few girls were educated except a handful in convent schools, training to be nuns. Girls from elite families received private tutoring.

Mexica woman cooking maize, from Florentine Codex.[lxxix]

Those who love Mexican food will be interested to know that it hasn't changed significantly from Aztec days. The Aztec diet was mostly plant-based: maize (corn), beans, tomatoes, guacamole, squash, and chilis. They made tortillas and tamales – just like today – and would occasionally have fish or wild game. Some areas raised domesticated dogs for consumption.

The biggest change the Spaniards brought to the Aztec diet was dairy products and meat from domesticated animals, like cattle, chickens, pigs, ducks, and goats. The Aztecs didn't have farm animals, so this was something new for them. They started making cheese from cow and goat milk, and that's why our tacos have cheese on them today! The Spaniards also brought banana plants, sugar cane, rice, olive oil, garlic, and other spices. The Spanish friars tried to suppress the use of hallucinogenic mushrooms used by the Aztecs in their religious ceremonies, but that quietly persisted into modern times.

The institution of marriage saw changes following Spanish control, especially among the nobility. In Aztec culture, men married in their early twenties, and women married around age 16. Parents arranged marriages, sometimes using a matchmaker. Young people from elite families could only marry other nobles and were often pawns in their families' schemes to create masterful alliances with other important families.

Even though their marriages were arranged, couples had a measure of autonomy in that when their first son was born, they could decide if they wanted to remain in the marriage or go their separate ways. Adultery was punishable by death in the city-state of Texcoco and some other cities. Ordinary Aztec men usually had just one wife, but higher-class men could have multiple wives and concubines. The tlatoani and especially the Huey Tlatoani were known for harems of many wives and concubines.

When the Spaniards converted the Aztecs to Catholicism, they forbade polygamy. They forced the tlatoani of Chalco and other nobility to choose one wife to keep and abandon the rest. Secondary wives and their children had no legal recognition in the new Spanish rule. The children were considered illegitimate and disinherited from property and rank.

The Spaniards didn't practice what they preached when it came to monogamy. Thousands of Spaniards – mostly men – flooded New Spain in the next two centuries. Many were single, and very few of the married men brought their wives and children. The single men often married the indigenous women or lived out-of-wedlock with them. The married men took mistresses from among the Aztec women. A case in point is Cortés himself.

Cortés was married to Catalina Suarez Marcayda when he arrived in Mexico but left her behind in Cuba. Shortly after Cortés arrived in Mexico, he acquired a slave-woman, Doña Marina, as both his translator and mistress, promising Marina he would release her from slavery if she would help him with Moctezuma. Cortés's wife, Catalina, joined him in 1522; three months later, she died suddenly, after an angry outburst regarding Doña Marina, now pregnant with Cortés's son, Martin. Charges of murder were brought against Cortés but dropped. When Marina gave birth, Cortés acknowledged Martin as his son and legitimized him in 1529.

Also, in 1529, he married a Spanish noblewoman Doña Juana de Zúñiga, but shortly before, Cortés helped himself to Doña Isabel, the daughter of Moctezuma II. Isabel had been the exceptionally young bride of two Aztec emperors. After her father's death, she was quickly married to her uncle Cuitlahuac, the new Huey Tlatoani. That marriage lasted 80 days before he died of smallpox. His cousin, Cuauhtémoc, then became emperor – and married Doña Isabel.

Five years later, Cortés executed Isabel's husband, the last Aztec emperor, then gave her in marriage to his friend Alonso de Grado, who died just a few months later. At that point, Cortés took Isabel into his own house. What happened next – either rape or seduction – left Isabel pregnant with Cortés's daughter. To cover his indiscretion and leave himself free to marry Doña Juana, Cortes quickly married Isabel off to another friend, Pedro Gallego de Andrade; Leonor Cortés-Moctezuma was born about five months later. Isabel wanted nothing to do with the baby, suggesting Leonor was the product of rape. Cortés gave her to a distant relative to raise, but provided for her care and included her in his will.

Mestizo child.[xxx]

What Cortés did to Marina and Isabel (and probably other indigenous women) was repeated thousands of times by other Spanish men. Whether raped, enslaved, wives, or mistresses, thousands of Aztec women gave birth to children with Spanish fathers. These children were called *Mestizos,* a category in the caste system of colonial Mexico. The Spanish government imposed the complex caste system, which determined a person's legal and social status. The priest decided a child's caste at baptism.

Caste depended on two basic factors: where a person was born and who the parents were. The four fundamental tiers (and there were many more) were:

> Peninsular: a full-blooded Spaniard born in Spain,
>
> Criollos: a full-blooded Spaniard born in the colonies,
>
> Mestizo: a person of mixed Spanish and indigenous ancestry, and
>
> Indios: an indigenous person of Mexico.

One's caste determined one's vocation, rank, and ability to accumulate wealth. Only Peninsulars could hold the highest administrative and church positions. Mestizos were not permitted to attend university, enter the priesthood, hold government positions, or be included in the goldsmith or other artisan guilds. The system generated discontent among the lower castes and eventually led to the Mexican War of Independence in 1810.

PART FOUR:
ART, CULTURE, & LEGACY

Chapter 13: The Aztec Religion

When the Mexica left their homeland of Aztlan, they were accompanied by their patron Huitzilopochtli, the blood-thirsty hummingbird god. Over the centuries, as they incorporated other deities from the cultures they encountered, they accumulated an immense array of gods and goddesses. Because the Aztecs freely appropriated the gods of other tribes as their own, sometimes their deities would have overlapping identities. For instance, the feathered serpent, Quetzalcoatl, was the god of wind, creation, and rain, but Tlaloc was also the god of the rain, and Ometeotl and Coatlicue were creator deities.

The functions and attributes of the pantheon of Aztec gods were fluid. The Nahuatl word *teotl* is usually translated as *god,* but it can also mean *sacred power.* Some scholars argue that we ought not to categorize these gods as discrete personalities (as with Greek and Roman gods) but as pantheistic forces or powers moving through the cosmos. For example, Tlaloc might be understood as the force or power associated with rain rather than a god.

H. B. Nicholson, a scholar of Aztec culture, classified their gods into three groups. The first group, *Celestial Creators,* included Ometeotl (creator of the universe) and Coatlicue (goddess of Aztlan, creator of the moon and stars, and mother of

Huitzilopochtli). The most important god in the second group, *Rain & Agricultural Fertility Gods*, was Tlaloc, god of rain and storms. The third group, *War-Sacrifice/Nourishment of the Sun & Earth Gods,* contained Quetzalcoatl (god of wind, air, and learning), Huitzilopochtli (god of war and the sun), Mictlantecuhtli (god of the underworld), Mixcoatl (god of the hunt, ancestor of the Toltecs, father of Quetzalcoatl), and Tezcatlipoca (god of the night and sorcery).

Model of the dual temples of Tlaloc and Huitzilopochtli on the Templo Mayor pyramid.[lxxxi]

When the Spaniards arrived in the Aztec capital of Tenochtitlan, they observed dual shrines on the top of the largest pyramid (Templo Mayor), where the gods Tlaloc and Huitzilopochtli were worshiped. A temple in the plaza facing the Templo Mayor was devoted to Ehecatl, god of the wind and a manifestation of Quetzalcoatl. These were the three of the four most important Aztec gods.

The fourth of the important gods was Huitzilopochtli's powerful ally, the Toltec god Tezcatlipoca. He was known as the *Adversary* and the *Enemy of Both Sides.* In Toltec mythology, he was the brother of Quetzalcoatl – but also his enemy. Although he could forgive sins, heal sickness, and deliver a man from his ordained fate, he was unlikely to do anything good for anyone due to his arbitrary nature. He was more likely to bring drought and famine. The Aztecs called him *He Whose Slaves We Are.*

Aztec religion pervaded all tiers of society. The Aztec state was a theocracy, with politics and religion intertwined. The kings presided as priests over the monthly festivals and state ceremonies, with the burden of stabilizing both the political and cosmic worlds. All citizens participated in daily rites. Cortés wrote that the people would burn incense in their temples every morning before beginning their work for the day. He said sometimes they practiced bloodletting, where they would cut their bodies and let the blood flow over their idols and sprinkle it around the temples.

In a deity impersonation ritual, the priests would choose a young warrior without any defect to be *ixiptla,* becoming a certain god for a season. The Aztecs believed this person actually became that god – and would be clothed as that god – receiving honor and food and female consorts for up to a year. He would be worshiped until the inevitable day came to be sacrificed.

Aztec rituals often reenacted their myths. The Templo Mayor symbolizes one of the greatest myths associated with Huitzilopochtli. When he was in his mother's womb, Coatlicue, his sister, Coyolxauhqui, and her 400 brothers attacked their mother. Just at that moment, Huitzilopochtli emerged from the womb to defend his mother, fully grown and armed for battle. He killed his sister, decapitated her, and threw her down Mount Coatepec. As her body bounced to the bottom of the mountain, it broke into pieces, while her head flew into the sky and became the moon. Huitzilopochtli also ate the hearts of his 400 half-brothers.

Monolithic stone representing the dismembered body of Coyolxauhqui after Huitzilopochtli decapitated her and flung her down the mountain.[lxxxii]

In 1978, electrical workers digging at the Templo Mayor pyramid base discovered an enormous monolithic stone representing Coyolxauhqui's dismembered body. This huge round stone was at the foot of the stairs leading up the Huitzilopochtli's temple. The pyramid symbolized the slopes of Mount Coatepec with the body of his sister at the bottom. At the top, the hearts of sacrificial victims were offered to Huitzilopochtli to eat.

The Aztecs followed two calendars. One was the natural 365-day solar calendar, and the other was a religious calendar of 260 days broken into units of 20 days. Each unit had its own gods with accompanying festivals and rituals. For instance, children would be sacrificed during the festival of *Atlcahualo,* honoring Tlaloc, god of rain. The next month would be the festival of *Tlacaxipehualiztli,* where captives would be flayed, and the priests would wear the victim's skin for 20 days.

Every 52 years, the two calendars aligned, and this was celebrated by the extravaganza of the New Fire ceremony. In the months and years leading up to the 52-year ceremony, the pyramid temples would be enlarged and made higher. In preparation, the people would rid their homes of their old clothing, cooking utensils, and other household goods to renew their lives for the new 52-year cycle.

All fires would be quenched at sunset as the priests marched up to the summit of Mount Huizachtecatl, a volcanic mountain on the eastern shore of Lake Texcoco that could be seen by the cities around the lake. The priests sacrificed a victim on the top of the mountain and lit a fire on his chest. That fire lit a nearby bonfire, signifying the new 52-year cycle. Runners lit torches from the bonfire and carried them down the mountain to light fires in the temples and homes.

Aztecs raised dogs, eagles, jaguars, and deer to sacrifice to their gods. Butterflies and hummingbirds were sacrificed to Quetzalcoatl. Self-sacrifice and bloodletting were also common. People would use the thorny tips of the agave plant to pierce their ear lobes, tongues, or genitals, or they would stab themselves with knives. If they caught themselves speaking hurtful words or listening to gossip, they would slit their tongues or ears to rid themselves of the malevolent spirit. For more serious sins, they would strangle themselves or jump off cliffs.

A priest was known as a *giver of things,* and his duty was to give the gods what they were owed through sacrifices, offerings, and ceremonies. The tlatoani of Tenochtitlan was the priest-king of Huitzilopochtli, attending state rituals in the main temples. The

Aztec Empire had two high priests who governed the pilgrimage centers of Cholula and Tenochtitlan; they were something like archbishops and even ministered outside the Aztec territory. Under these two men were many levels of priests, priestesses, monks, and nuns who tended the shrines of their deities.

Cortés wrote that temples and shrines were found in every district of Tenochtitlan and the suburbs. He said that living quarters for the priests were next to the shrines. The priests wore black clothing and never cut or combed their hair from the time they entered the priesthood until they left it. The sons of nobles and respected citizens were placed in the temple around age seven or eight, living there as novices and celibate priests until their parents arranged a marriage for them. They were allowed no contact with women and had to abstain from certain foods.

In the *Florentine Codex*, Franciscan friar Sahagún wrote of folk healers or shamans who traveled from place to place, tending to both spiritual and physical ailments and using psychedelic mushrooms and other plants to treat patients. He also mentioned enchanters who dealt with black magic and the occult, grinding the seeds of the morning glory plant to make *Ololiuqui* tea, which brought visions. Sahagún described Ololiuqui intoxication as troubling, making one deranged or possessed, where the person saw terrifying things.

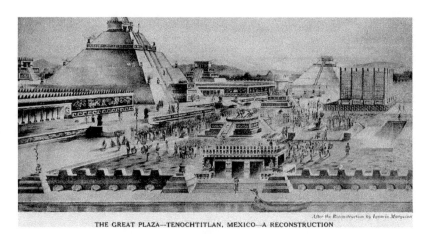

THE GREAT PLAZA—TENOCHTITLAN, MEXICO—A RECONSTRUCTION

The main temple complex in Tenochtitlan.[lxxiii]

In front of every major temple was a large courtyard where people gathered to sing, dance, watch the religious rituals, enjoy psychedelic mushrooms, and drink chocolate. Caught up in the tempo of the shrieking flutes and pounding drums, the people would pierce themselves and sprinkle their blood toward the idols. The *calli* (temples) were dimly lit by the coals burning incense, filling the darkness with smoke. The floor was covered with flowers and slippery with the blood of sacrifices. In alcoves around the temple's perimeter sat the idols on their pedestals, swathed in jewels, veils, feathers, and bells.

In a letter to the King of Spain, Cortés wrote of one special temple in Tenochtitlan, probably the Templo Mayor:

> "Among these temples there is one which far surpasses all the rest, for within its precincts, surrounded by a lofty wall, there is room enough for a town of five hundred families. Around the interior of this enclosure there are handsome edifices, containing large halls and corridors, in which the religious persons attached to the temple reside. There are full forty towers, which are lofty and well built, the largest of which has fifty steps leading to its main body and is higher than the tower of e principal church at Seville. . .

The interior of the chapels containing the idols consists of curious imagery, wrought in stone with plaster ceilings and woodwork carved in relief and painted with figures of monsters and other objects. Every chapel in them is dedicated to a particular idol, to which they pay their devotions. There are three halls in this grand temple, which contain the principal idols; leading from the halls are chapels with very small doors, to which the light is not admitted, nor are any persons except the priests, and not all of them."

Prisoner led to the top of a pyramid for sacrifice.[lxxxiv]

Aztecs believed that the human body was a sacred reservoir of divine forces, with the ability to release its energy back into the cosmos. The head and hair contained *tonalli,* an energy responsible for the body's strength and health. The heart contained *teyolia,* tied to human reasoning and perception. It was like a divine fire, especially strong in priests. When a person died, the *teyolia* left the body, and when a warrior died, his teyolia rose to the sun. Aztecs perceived human sacrifice as a means of recycling energy. The energy released from the sacrificial victims nourished the gods, who then nourished humans through rain, food, and other provision. About 20,000 people became the victims of sacrifice each year in different types of ceremonial rituals.

Some sacrifices mimicked the dismemberment of Huitzilopochtli's sister, Coyolxuahqui, cutting off the arms and thighs of the victim. An infamous sacrifice was practiced during the annual festival of Toxcatl, celebrating the *smoking mirror* god Tezcatlipoca. This was a god-impersonating ritual involving a young warrior in perfect condition, who lived for one year as the god *Tezcatlipoca*. Before and during the killing, the people gathered in the vast plaza of the Templo Mayor, piercing themselves until the pavement ran with blood. As the priests carried out the phases of the rituals, the people jumped and twirled to percussive music, led by dancers in striking costumes. After the young man was killed, the priest would add his head to the skull rack. The skull rack represented the divine force of tonalli, which resided in the head.

Beginning in 2015, The National Institute of Anthropology and History collected about 200 skulls from the *tzompantli* (skull rack) in the Templo Mayor area. Analysis of the skulls showed that 75% of the skulls found were young men of warrior age, while 20% were women and 5% were children. The size of the tower that supported the skull rack suggests that thousands of skulls were displayed.

This jaguar-like stone vessel was used to hold the hearts of sacrificial victims.[lxxxv]

Huitzilopochtli, the hummingbird god, taught the Mexica about human sacrifice after they left Aztlan. Once they established the Triple Alliance with other Aztec tribes, their god demanded nourishment from a recurring and increasing supply of the blood, hearts, and other body parts of human victims. The priests would push and drag the victim to the god's shrine on top of the Templo Mayor pyramid, where four priests tied the victim and held him in place on a sacrificial table. The high priest (or the tlatoani) would stab the victim in the upper abdomen, quickly reach under the rib cage, rip the heart out of the body, and hold it up – still beating – before the image of Huitzilopochtli. The priest or king then placed the heart in the jaguar vessel, or the basin held by the chac mool figurine. The viscera were fed to the animals in Moctezuma's zoo. Sometimes ritual cannibalism took place, eating the thighs and arms of the victim.

Chac Mool, from Templo Mayor, holding a basin used to receive blood or the heart of a sacrificial victim.[lxxxvi]

Next to Huitzilopochtli's temple on top of the Templo Mayor pyramid stood the matching temple of the rain god Tlaloc, who demanded the tears of children; small children from noble families were offered by their parents. The *Codex Ixtlilxochitl* estimated that 20% of Aztec children were sacrificed every year; their tears dripping to the ground would cause Tlaloc to drip rain on the soil in the planting season. The *Codex Magliabecchi* records children sacrificed by drowning and mentions two instances of the sacrifice of newborn babies. According to this codex, five of the 18 festivals of the Aztec religious year included child sacrifice.

In 2008, archeologists analyzed the skeletons of 31 children found in the excavation of Temple R in Tlatelolco (just next to Tenochtitlan), dedicated to Ehecatl-Quetzalcoatl, the Toltec-Aztec god of wind and rain. Two-thirds of the children were infants and toddlers, mostly little boys. Archeological evidence indicates they were all killed in a single ceremony, most likely during the great drought of AD 1454–57.

Some vestiges of Aztec religion have endured through the colonial period and until the present day. Aztecs in northern Veracruz still worship a god called Ometotiotsij, who is probably Ometeotl, the creator god. Mexicans celebrate the *Day of the Dead* by incorporating indigenous rites associated with the god of the underworld, Mictlantecuhtli, and his wife, Mictecacihuatl.

The practice of *curanderismo* (traditional folk medicine) goes back to Aztec days and is widespread in Mexico today. Traditional healers are especially important if the illness appears to result from witchcraft. Healers are believed to have spiritual power and use prayers and chanting of incantations, offerings of incense and food, various herbs, and occasionally blood from a sacrificed chicken.

A few Mexicans in the Pueblo region east of Mexico City (former Aztec and Totonac region) still worship the sun god Tonatiuh (a manifestation of Quetzalcoatl), which they call *Jesús* in Spanish. In the early colonial days, the Franciscan friars taught the people about Jesus, with passages like Luke 1:78 about the "rising sun will come to us from heaven." In the Aztec mind, Tonatiuh became Jesus – also known as *the Solar Christ*.

Dancers in the December 12 feast day of Our Lady of Guadalupe, in front of her Basilica.[lxxxvii]

Tonantzin was an Aztec goddess called *mother earth* and *honored grandmother*. She became associated with the Virgin Mary. The Basilica of Guadalupe was built to honor the Virgin Mary (after several visions of Mary to two men, where she appeared as an Aztec princess). The shrine was built on a site where a temple to Tonantzin had stood and is the most-visited Catholic shrine in the world. Our Lady of Guadalupe is also known as the Queen of Mexico. The Aztecs transmitted their worship of Tonantzin to the Virgin of Guadalupe in the same way that they syncretized the teachings and rituals of Catholicism with their Aztec worldview and religion.

Chapter 14: Crafts, Commerce and Social Life

Everything fell apart when the Spaniards arrived. Until that time, Aztecs lived in a distinctly stratified society, unified by a common quest to expand their empire and spread their religion. The trading class was reaching its zenith when Cortés invaded, and merchants were gaining wealth comparable to the aristocracy. Would the powerful middle-class merchants and traders have eventually broken the strict barriers of the ruling class, generating a more fluid stratification? One can only speculate how the great Aztec Empire might have evolved.

An Aztec baby's destiny mostly depended on his or her parents: their lineage and where they stood in the clearly defined social hierarchy. At the top were the nobility, including political leaders, judges, priests, and military commanders. Next were the artisans, architects, merchants, traders, and lower administrative officials. Under them were construction workers, laborers, and farmers, and finally, there were slaves. Young people had limited opportunity to rise above their parents' social position unless they demonstrated unusual merit.

There were four ways to become a *tlachohtin* (slave*)* in Aztec society. A child or adult could be captured in war or sent as tribute from conquered city-states. The adults were often sacrificed, but children, beautiful women, and some men were kept as slaves. Sometimes criminals were sentenced to slavery. If someone gambled too much and got into deep debt, they could sell themselves. Slavery wasn't always lifelong; one could buy their freedom. Slaves rarely were resold by their masters unless they had the slave's agreement.

Slaves were used for farm labor and construction work and as household servants; beautiful women slaves were purchased to be concubines for the nobility. Slaves who were educated or skilled or who learned quickly could be promoted to higher positions, such as managing their owner's estate or business. They could even own other slaves! Aztec law protected slaves from abuse (other than human sacrifice) and permitted slaves to marry free citizens. Slavery was not inherited; children born to slaves were free.

The largest group in Aztec society were farmers (*macehualtin*). At the lower level were laborers who plowed the fields, planted, watered, weeded, and harvested. Above them were the specialists, who implemented crop rotation, oversaw the construction of the floating gardens and terraced fields, and supervised seeding, transplanting, and harvesting. All farmers were expected to join the military campaigns in the lull between harvesting and planting, and the field laborers assisted with building roads and temples in the off-season.

Irrigation, from Florentine Codex[lxxxviii]

Aztecs enjoyed successful agricultural endeavors, even without horses or mules to help with plowing or pulling loads. Some parts of the empire were well-watered, but others needed irrigation, especially in dry seasons or times of drought. The farmers of Mesoamerica had used irrigation systems for centuries, but the Aztecs took it to a higher level with more complex and extensive canals, even diverting rivers to meet their needs. The Aztec city-states around Lake Texcoco were in a mountainous region, so they built terraces up the hills and mountains, where seeds could be planted on level ground.

Chinampas ("floating" gardens) were widely used to cultivate vegetables and flowers. These were constructed by dredging mud up from the lake bottom and alternating that with vegetative matter until they had small rectangular islands where they could grow crops. These island beds had a network of canals running through them for the farmers to access by canoe. The chinampas were so fertile they could grow seven crops a year; seedlings were started on rafts and then transplanted. Tenochtitlan itself had a chinampas system, but its huge population relied on the extensive chinampas of Lake Xochimilco to the south and connected to Lake Texcoco. Farmers in Xochimilco transported produce and flowers by boat to Tenochtitlan and other cities in the lake system.

The Aztecs were exceptionally proud of their artisans, which they called *tolteca* in honor of the highly esteemed Toltec civilization which preceded the Aztecs and became part of their lineage through intermarriage. Skilled Aztec craftsmen were greatly respected and created their amazing carpentry, pottery, metalwork, stone carvings, and other crafts in large workshops. These educated craftworkers executed measurements using geometry and used tools made from copper and obsidian to carve and sculpt stone and wood.

An important craftwork for artisans was building weapons for the warfare that defined the Aztecs. They crafted 6-foot-long blowguns with darts tipped with secretions from poisonous frogs, built war clubs with embedded razor-like obsidian blades and axes with heads of stone or copper, and crafted daggers with beautifully carved hilts from flint or obsidian.

Boatbuilding was an essential craft because Tenochtitlan was an island on a large lake connected to other lakes. Aztecs used the waterways to travel from one city to another and to navigate the canal system interlacing the Tenochtitlan neighborhoods. Flat-bottomed dug-out canoes were used for gardening the chinampas and transportation through the canals, the mainland, and around the lake. The Aztecs also built rafts of planks tied with tight fibers for transporting large objects, such as stone figurines. Engineers and craftsmen were required to design and build canals, dikes, and aqueducts for transportation, managing fluctuating water levels, and delivering fresh drinking water.

Carpenters crafted homes and temples from wood, stone, or adobe bricks with thatched or slate roofs. Aztec stone masons covered the outside of buildings with limestone plaster and carved intricate designs on the front of temples and palaces. Homes held generations of families in rooms built around a central courtyard.

Architects and city planners meticulously devised the plan for the capital city of Tenochtitlan before it was built. With an estimated population of 200,000, the city had four quadrants, each housing around 50,000 people, surrounding the ceremonial center where the main temples were located. Each quadrant was divided into four smaller districts of 10,000 to 15,000 people. These smaller districts were called *calpolli*, like the estates in the countryside, as they each had their own leadership, their own central plaza with a temple and marketplace, and they often specialized in specific craftsmanship – such as pottery or feather work. A canal system served as the major streets through the city, connecting to the surrounding lake.

Mural by Diego Rivera in Palacio Nacional, Mexico City, showing life in Aztec times. In the forefront is the market of Tlatelolco, with the pochteca tlatoque presiding. In the background is the island city of Tenochtitlan with its causeway and canal system.[lxxix]

Merchants and traders accumulated significant wealth and power in the organized and diverse marketplaces of the Aztec Empire. In neighborhood market centers located in each calpolli, *tlacuilo* (merchants) sold precious metals and gems, cotton cloth and clothing, animal hides, vegetables and fruit, wild game, intricate carvings, utensils for the home, and much more. The marketplace drw people together to gossip, share the local news, and learn of important events in the empire.

The *pochteca* (long-distance traders) enjoyed great prestige as they traveled great distances to obtain the coveted goods of the nobility. This was a hereditary position and could bring great wealth. Still, the pochteca were not permitted to display their prosperity by wearing the feathers and rich clothing of nobility. The fine cotton prized by elite Aztecs needed to be grown below an elevation of 5000 feet; it could not be grown in the mountainous regions around Tenochtitlan. Thus, Aztecs had to trade for cotton grown in distant regions or conquer the area and require them to pay cotton as tribute. The pochteca also acquired cacao beans for chocolate, colorful bird feathers, gems, gold, and animal skins. Because the Aztecs did not use beasts of burden, all these goods had to be transported in boats down the rivers or by porters over land.

The *pochteca tlatoque* served as overseers of the traders. These were the most experienced and accomplished traders who supervised the markets and held court to administer justice to those in the trader class. Another group of long-distance traders called the *naualoztomeca* traveled to hostile territories in disguise; they were spies for the state, picking up information as they interacted with people in the frontier areas.

The *tlaltani* traders specialized in the slave trade, an important source of sacrificial victims. The *tencunenenque* collected tribute in the city-states around the empire. The *Codex Mendoza* details the astounding quantities of goods the tencunenenque collected, such as textiles, grain, feathers, honey, jade, and copper. In a list of tribute from one town, the *Codex Mendoza* recorded they were required to send 1200 bales of cotton each year, and every six months, they would send:

- 800 loads of red and white cloaks with ornamental borders of green, yellow, red, and blue
- 400 loads of lioncloths
- 400 loads of large white cloaks

All this clothing required the women to spend most of their days weaving cloth to meet the tribute demands.

All teenage boys were trained in warfare, and able-bodied adult men had to maintain that training and be prepared to mobilize in the huge military campaigns. However, the Aztecs operated a standing army of the best warriors, who had received advanced training as teens or distinguished themselves on the battlefield. They could come from any class. The warrior class was highly honored and a channel for upward mobility. Social risers in the warrior class were called *eagle nobles.*

The priestly class organized the religious rituals and festivals, ran the mandatory education system, and controlled the artisans. Some priests specialized in astronomy, medicine, or prophecy. Priests also served as warriors, carrying the effigies of their gods and capturing enemy warriors for sacrifice. Anyone from any class could become a priest, but priests in leadership came from noble families.

Aztec nobility, wearing elaborate feather headdresses, brightly colored capes, earrings, and lip piercings. From folio 65 of the Codex Mendoza.[xc]

Tlatoani (kings) and *Huey Tlatoani* (emperors) were elected by the *pipiltin* (nobility). The pipiltin were private landowners, usually of large estates, and formed the ruling councils for the city-states. They were distinguished by their clothing of finest cotton, multiple piercings (nose, ears, tongue, lips), and bright feather capes and headdresses. Teteuhctin served as city and regional governors, lived in grand palaces, and were honored by the *-tzin* suffix at the end of their names.

From the top down, the political structure of the Aztec Empire started with the Huey Tlatoani (emperor). At the beginning of the Triple Alliance, the rulers of Tenochtitlan, Texcoco, and Tlacopan took turns serving as Huey Tlatoani, but eventually, Tenochtitlan provided top leadership. Under him were the tlatoani (kings) of the *altepetls* or city-states (which had smaller cities and towns under their rule). These were broken down into the calpolli, usually kinship units, which were farming villages in the rural areas and neighborhood districts in the big cities.

The altepetls constantly endeavored to gain ascendency over their neighbor city-states through warfare, so they could enrich themselves from tributes they would receive. The altepetls were persistently forming alliances, some short-lived and others long-term, to defend themselves or conquer other regions. This is how the Aztec Triple Alliance was able to overthrow the dominant city of Azcapotzalco and exercise political hegemony (supremacy) over a large portion of Mesoamerica.

The fundamental unit of Aztec society was the family, to whom lineage was paramount. Nobles traced their lineage back to the Toltecs and from there back to Quetzalcoatl. The family tree of both parents was important, although the paternal lineage was foremost. Young men and women could only marry someone in their own social class; brides were expected to be virgins, and the young men were encouraged to be celibate before marriage. The wedding involved a four-day celebration with feasting and speeches; the bride would be covered in gold pyrite dust and adorned with red feathers.

Women were the keepers of the home: cooking, caring for the younger children, teaching their daughters, and weaving (lots of weaving). Aztec women could own their property and maintained control over any inheritance. With proper training before marriage, they could engage as healers, midwives, priestesses, and merchants. Aztec men were the primary wage earners, caregivers, and teachers of their sons once they reached three years old. Married couples lived with the husband's family in multigenerational homes.

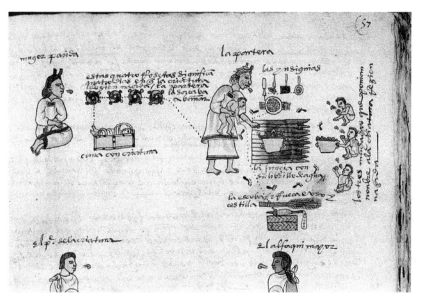

Aztec naming ceremony, from the Codex Mendoza. At the top left, the mother addresses her baby in its cradle. After four days, the midwife takes the baby for ritual bathing and naming (top right). On the right of this scene, three boys call out the name of the infant, and above and below it are symbols of possible future careers for boys and girls.[xci]

Four days after a baby was born, the family gathered for a naming ritual, something like a baptism. The midwife would bathe the infant outdoors in the early-morning sun, give the child a name and a gift that symbolized his or her future role in society. A baby girl would often get weaving equipment and a broom, and a boy might get arrows and a shield or utensils representing his father's trade. Babies received a calendar name based on the date of their naming ritual, along with a personal name. To get a more auspicious date for the calendar name, parents might adjust the naming day to the third or fifth day after birth.

The *Codex Mendoza* details the raising of children: their lessons, punishments, and how many tortillas they would eat at each age. Three-year-old boys and girls would get a half tortilla for a meal and eventually work up to two or three in their teens. Beginning at age three, mothers would teach their daughters the first steps in how to weave, and when they were in their early teens, they would learn how to cook. Women spent an inordinate amount of time weaving to keep up with the tribute demands; thus, much of a girl's training was in that area. Fathers took their sons along to teach them their trade; they taught them other skills such as gathering firewood, cutting reeds for making baskets, and fishing with nets.

Boys and girls received only verbal correction and scolding up to age eight. After that, if children were careless, disobedient, or disrespectful, parents would administer corporal punishment. Sometimes children would be pricked with maguey spines or forced to breathe in the smoke of roasting chili peppers.

Their calpolli leaders supervised the parental education of children. In addition to life skills, the children were expected to learn *huehuetlatolli (sayings of the old)*. These were polite greetings and short speeches for all sorts of occasions, such as saying goodbye to a dying person or celebrating the birth of a child. Occasionally, the children would have to report to their local temples to be tested on their training.

The Mexica were among the first people in the world to mandate compulsory education for both boys and girls of all classes. Around 14 or 15, boys from elite families attended a school for the nobility called *calmecac,* and commoners attended a *telpochcalli* (both described in chapter 12), where they lived in dormitories. Girls attended schools to learn to sing and dance but lived at home. The glorious goal of most boys was to serve their nation as great warriors. At age ten, boys got a short haircut with one lock left long in the back. They wore this hairstyle until they went into battle and captured their first prisoner, and then the lock was cut as a rite of passage.

The Aztecs worked hard, battled even harder, and participated in gruesome religious rituals. But their lives weren't always grim. They did take time to play. They engaged in a ball game –

something like basketball – called *Ullamaliztli Tlachtli*. They had to get a rubber ball (courtesy of the Olmec civilization) into a stone hoop but couldn't use their hands (like soccer). Instead, they used their hips, knees, elbows, and heads to keep the ball in the air (which skilled players could do for an hour or more). A lot of gambling was involved. Dancing and singing were sometimes for religious or political events, but also just for fun. Sometimes they would be accompanied by comic sketches.

Aztec board game called Patolli, from Florentine Codex by Bernardino de Sahagún.[xcii]

And then there were the pillow fights! They had this annual event where the boys would throw grass-filled sacks at the girls, and the girls would chase after them with cactus thorns. Teen boys would challenge rival schools to ballgames and mock battles. Adults and young people enjoyed "board games" on reed mats, using beans for dice.

Let's not forget the zoo! When the conquistadors entered Tenochtitlan, one thing that grabbed their attention was a garden full of plants and strange animals – creatures they had never seen. Many wrote more about the zoo than anything else in the city. They said it was so huge that it took 300 keepers to tend the animals.

The Spaniards didn't know the names of all the animals but listed bears, eagles, wolves, and monkeys, describing what were probably jaguar, ocelot, puma, sloths, armadillos, crocodiles, flamingos, and many other birds, and even a bison! The zoo was located on palace grounds, so it was probably reserved for the nobility to enjoy. It wasn't the only zoo either! One conquistador, Bernal Díaz de Castillo, said he saw another one across the lake in Texcoco.

Chapter 15: Aztec Art

Thoughts of Aztec culture often conjure up images of bold and colorful art. Ancient preexisting cultures influenced the flamboyant artistry of the Aztecs – the civilizations they conquered and bordering civilizations with whom they traded. In turn, the Aztecs used their art as a sort of propaganda, exerting their dominance over the city-states of their vast empire. Through military conquest, the Aztecs achieved political dominance and cultural hegemony over their tributary civilizations.

During the 20 years that the migrating Mexica lived in the ruins of Tula, they reverenced the Toltec art and craftsmanship, striving to emulate this spectacular culture, even calling their own artisans *tolteca.* The Mexica also learned from the cultures of the Olmec, Maya, Zapotec, Huastecs, and others. From Oaxaca in the southern reaches of their empire, they imported a community of artists to Tenochtitlan. They combined the diverse artistry of multiple civilizations into their own eclectic style of painting, jewelry, sculptures, ceramics, metalwork, architecture, and more. Grotesque and abstract carvings incongruously existed side-by-side with graceful, naturalistic imagery of humans and animals.

Aztec writing was an art form; however, with no alphabet, it wasn't a fully developed writing system. They combined pictographs with signs that represented sounds. For example, *ma* was the word for *hand*. To write a word with the sound *ma* in it, they would use the picture for hand. If they had a word ending in *tlan* (like Aztlan), they would use the picture for tooth (*tlantli*).

Travel from one place to another was shown by footprints. Travel through time was indicated by dotted lines and number symbols. Speech was shown by *speech scrolls* in front of a person's mouth. Examples of all three are in the previous chapter's picture of the baby's naming ceremony.

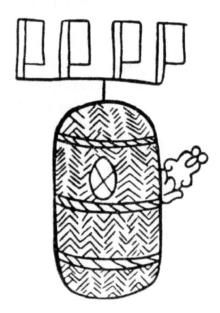

Aztec glyph or pictograph for 80 bales of cacao beans (for chocolate). Each of the four flags at the top represents the number 20. The oval picture on the bale represents cacao beans. (From the Book of Tributes.)[xciii]

The Aztecs also had a *vigesimal* system (based on the number 20) for writing numerals. One dot (or sometimes a finger) represented 1. Two dots meant 2; 5 was represented by a bar, while 6 was a bar and one dot. Two bars meant 10, and 11 was two bars and a dot, while 20 was a flag, and 21 was a flag and one dot. The hundreds were represented by a feather with a certain number of barbs, each representing 20 units.

Writing and painting require something to write on, so the Aztecs had *amate* paper made from the Amate tree, a type of Ficus. Amate paper was used primarily for codices (manuscripts) and widely used in the Triple Alliance for communication, tribute records, and rituals. Forty villages (in what is now the state of Morelos) produced about 480,000 sheets of paper annually, which they sent as tribute to the Triple Alliance cities. The paper was made by soaking the bark overnight and then pounding it into sheets with volcanic stones.

Aztecs painted their distinctive art on amate paper, deerskin, cotton canvases, ceramics, wood, and stone. They would sometimes primer the surface with gesso, a mixture of rabbit-skin glue, chalk, and white pigment. The Aztecs commonly used coral, chalk, clay, and stone in paintings and drawings. Many of their paintings were codices; sadly, most of those were destroyed by the Spaniards immediately following the conquest. However, the Spanish government commissioned the *Codex Mendoza,* painted by Aztec artists, and allowed codices dealing with history or tribute payments to be produced.

Aztecs learned the art of painting murals from the remnants of the Teotihuacan culture. The Templo Mayor and other important buildings in Tenochtitlan were adorned with complex murals, depicting people in a similar style as in the codices. An old man and woman pictured in a mural in Tlatelolco (just next to Tenochtitlan) are believed to be Cipactonal and Oxomico, the first man and woman in the first world, something like Adam and Eve – except in Aztec cosmology, the first world didn't survive.

In 2002, archaeologists discovered an ancient cistern in Tlatelolco underneath a colonial church. This was built on the orders of Cuauhtémoc, the last emperor of the Aztecs, who had relocated there with the remnant of Tenochtitlan's citizens after the Spaniards conquered Tenochtitlan. The cistern was 7-feet-deep and 26-feet-wide and was fed from an aqueduct that flowed four miles from Chapultepec Hill. The cistern walls were painted with brightly colored frescos of fishermen casting their nets and people paddling their canoes. They are surrounded by ducks, frogs, herons, and jaguars in the reeds and water lilies of the lake.

"One Flower" ceremony celebrated with two drums, which are called the teponaztli (foreground) and the huehuetl (background). Florentine Codex.

Aztecs loved singing and poetry, and most festivals featured poetry contests, musical presentations, and acrobatic performances. Songs fell into several genres: *Yaocuicatl* was sung to the gods of war, *Teocuicatl* honored the gods of creation and conveyed creation myths, *Xochicuicatl* were songs of flowers used in a metaphorical sense.

Poetry was especially famous among the Acolhua tribe of the Aztecs, who often used parallelism and couplets with concrete concepts to metaphorically describe two perspectives of an abstract idea. For instance, the concept of poetry was expressed as *the flower, the song.* Fortunately, we can read this poetry today, as some of it was preserved by the descendants of the Acolhua royalty of Texcoco and Tepexpan. Here is a hymn by King Nezahualcoyotl of Texcoco:

YOU, AZURE BIRD

You, azure bird, shining parrot, you walk flying. Oh Highest Arbiter, Life Giver: trembling, You extend Yourself here, filling my house, filling my dwelling, here.

Ohuaya, Ohuaya!

With Your piety and grace one can live, oh Author of Life, on earth: trembling,

You extend Yourself here, filling my house, filling my dwelling, here. Ohuaya, Ohuaya!

Aztecs are renowned for their remarkable stone sculpturing, which varied from exquisite miniature figurines to colossal monuments. Aztec sculptures featured realistic carvings of snakes, jaguars, frogs, monkeys, and other animals, as well as massive figures of their deities, encrusted with jewels and layers of gold. Although most carvings preserved through the centuries now appear the color of the stone they were carved from, they were brightly painted and decorated when they were new.

Replica of Aztec Sunstone painted in what scholars believe were the original colors.[xciv]

A striking example of Aztec sculpture, the enormous *Sunstone* or *Calendarstone* was uncovered in 1790 in the area that once was Templo Mayor in Tenochtitlan. Carved from basalt around 1427, it measures about 12 feet in diameter and 3 feet thick. What is probably the face of the sun-god Tonatiuh grimaces from the middle of the disk, surrounded by four squares representing four of the five suns that consecutively replaced each other through the millennia.

Stone of Moctezuma I, where human gladiators were chained for a battle to the death.[xcv]

Two unique Aztec sculpture forms are related to the culture of human sacrifice. One is the *cuauhxicalli,* a large stone bowl usually shaped like a jaguar or eagle and used to hold human hearts after sacrifice (see the photo of jaguar cuauhxicalli in chapter 13). The other is the *temalacatl,* a huge stone disk on which two captured warriors stood to fight in one-to-one combat until the death, another form of human sacrifice. Two famous examples of temalacatl stones are the *Stone of Moctezuma I* and the *Stone of Tizoc.*

In 1790, some men building a water canal in central Mexico City discovered a gruesome statue of the goddess Coatlicue. Coatlicue was the earth-mother goddess who lived on Mount Coatepec on Aztlan and the mother of Huitzilopochtli, the hummingbird god. The almost 9-foot-tall statue shows a decapitated woman with two coral snakes representing blood spurting from her neck. (In one version of Huitzilopochtli's birth, her head was cut off by her daughter Coyolxauhqui). Around her neck, she wears a garland of human hands and hearts and a human skull pendant. Her skirt is writhing rattlesnakes, and she has claws for hands and feet to rip into human corpses.

Colossal statue of goddess Coatlicue.[xcvi]

Aztecs believed she would devour the human population if the sun failed to rise, and since that was Huitzilopochtli's job, they were sure to keep him well-fed with sacrifices. After she was dug up, the statue of the goddess was moved to the University of Mexico to be studied. But the professors were worried the locals might start worshiping her again, so that they reburied her, right there on the college campus. In 1803, a visiting scholar dug her up to make drawings and a cast, but he found her so disturbing that he buried her again when he was done. Finally, scholars dug her up for the last time in 1823, and she has managed to stay above ground since, at the National Museum of Anthropology in Mexico City.

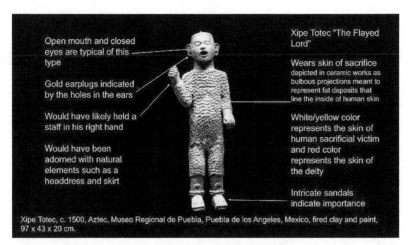

Open mouth and closed eyes are typical of this type

Gold earplugs indicated by the holes in the ears

Would have likely held a staff in his right hand

Would have been adorned with natural elements such as a headdress and skirt

Xipe Totec "The Flayed Lord"

Wears skin of sacrifice depicted in ceramic works as bulbous projections meant to represent fat deposits that line the inside of human skin

White/yellow color represents the skin of human sacrificial victim and red color represents the skin of the deity

Intricate sandals indicate importance

Xipe Totec, c. 1500, Aztec, Museo Regional de Puebla, Puebla de los Angeles, Mexico, fired clay and paint, 97 x 43 x 20 cm.

Small statue of Xipe Totec.[xcvii]

Throughout the Valley of Mexico, smaller stone statues have been discovered in rural areas. These are the gods of agriculture and local deities. A common smaller sculpture is that of Xipe Totec, the maize god, otherwise known as the *Flayed Lord.* Worshiped by the Toltecs and later the Aztecs, he wore the flayed skin of a human sacrifice victim as a symbol of new vegetation.

This pendant carved from jade of Chalchiutlicue (Jade Skirt), a young goddess, is about 2 3/4 x 1 3/8 inches in size.[xcviii]

Artisans also carved tiny sculptures of precious materials, such as amethyst, turquoise, conch shell, rock crystal, and jade. These miniature carvings were usually worn as pendants or earrings.

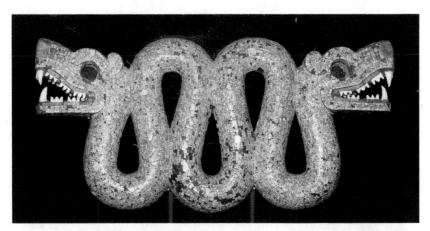

Double-headed mosaic turquoise serpent.[xcix]

Aztec artists loved the blue-green color of the turquoise stone and frequently used it in a mosaic form on sculptures and masks. On display in the British Museum is a beautiful double-headed snake carved from a single piece of cedarwood and covered in tiny squares of turquoise. His red mouth and nose are made from the spiny oyster spondylus, and conch shells form his teeth. He was probably worn as a chest ornament in special festivals. Why is he double-headed? In the Nahuatl language, the word *coatl* means *snake,* but it also means *twin,* carrying the idea of cooperation and friendship. X*iuhcoatl* means turquoise snake (or the fire serpent), which represents lightning, linking sky and earth.

Cholula Pottery:

Even without a potter's wheel, Aztec artisans formed beautiful ceramics, including urns for funeral ashes, jugs, cups, eating bowls and plates, cooking pots, mortar vessels for grinding chili peppers, goblets, and vases. Aztec ceramic pieces were usually thin (especially the Cholula pottery) and often featured black geometric designs on an orange background for everyday household pottery. Finer pieces had a cream, red, or black slip (a mixture of clay and water used to decorate ceramics) and might feature flower, leaf, or animal designs.

The artisans of Cholula were famous for their delicate ceramics, known as *Mixteca-Puebla* style, and these were imported to Tenochtitlan for Moctezuma and other nobles. In the early Aztec period, pottery was usually decorated with floral designs and glyphs representing days. Ceramics from the later period featured simple lines, sometimes curved or looped. Aztec pottery was formed in molds or carved from hard clay, then fired in updraft kilns or open-fired in pits at low temperatures.

Featherwork is a dazzling art form that is a classic feature of Aztec culture. Bird feathers in brilliant colors were collected to form intricate mosaics, decorate weapons, and weave into headdresses and capes. The most highly prized feathers were from the resplendent quetzal birds, which have long emerald-green tail feathers and scarlet breast feathers. They also used flamingo feathers and other brightly colored feathers, some harvested from the birds in Moctezuma's Zoo. A whole district in the capital city of Tenochtitlan housed the guild of the *Amanteca* feather artisans, who were not required to pay tribute or perform public service.

Moctezuma's headdress of quetzal feathers (reproduction).[a]

The Amanteca artisans would chop feathers into small pieces to use in mosaic art, or feather painting, on shields and cloaks for the idols. The mosaics usually were formed on a base of amate paper, sometimes covered with cotton and paste, and then they would use the precious feathers of the quetzal bird and other birds with striking colors, along with dyed feathers, all chopped up and adhered with glue made from orchid bulbs. Striking headdresses, cloaks, fly whisks, fans, and other decorative objects were made from whole feathers sewn in place with string made from the agave plant.

Metalworking in Mesoamerica had its origins in the Purépecha-Tarascan culture northwest of the Aztec lands, close to the Pacific Ocean. From there, elements of technique, form, and style diffused throughout Mesoamerica. The Mixtec civilization of Oaxaca and Pueblo were the dominant goldsmiths. The Mixtec became a tributary region of the Aztecs, and just the Aztecs imported Amanteca featherwork artisans into Tenochtitlan; they probably had a guild of Mixtec goldsmiths plying their trade as well.

Using borrowed technology, imported copper, gold, tin, and lead, and probably imported metallurgists, Aztec artisans manufactured elegant and sophisticated metallurgy. In their Tenochtitlan workshops, they created breath-taking castings of flowers and animals in gold and copper-gold, which were displayed in their pleasure gardens. Their artisans also cast hundreds of tin, arsenic bronze, and copper bells for the Templo Mayor.

The artisans worked the metal in furnaces with extremely high temperatures, where the flames were fanned by blowing air through pipes. They used molds to form metal objects and also hammered the metal into sheets. They implemented a technology called lost-wax casting to make bells and other objects. Aztec artisans were also known for their filigree work. Unfortunately, most of their gold artifacts were melted down by the conquistadors to make gold bricks for currency. Some smaller items survived, such as gold lip rings, earrings, and necklaces.

Just as their Olmec, Toltec, and Teotihuacan predecessors had done, the Aztecs utilized art to fortify their political and cultural supremacy. Their impressive pyramids and temples, their dramatic sculptures, and their exquisite mosaic art represented the central components of their religion. The dazzling and exotic featherwork, bejeweled carvings, and colossal monuments testified to their conquered city-states of the great might and affluence of the Aztec Empire and their right to dominate.

Even their paper imposed their influence on their subject city-states. The Amate paper, which was believed to have special powers, was used to record tribute from dominated cities and villages and became a representation of the transaction between the conquerors and the vanquished. Amate paper was used to register the fine cotton, turquoise, gold, long quetzal feathers, and other luxuries provided as tribute from the far reaches of the empire. Even the paper itself was produced by conquered people.

When the Aztecs conquered a new region, they permitted the people to continue worshiping their local deities, but they also imposed their own religion – worship of Huitzilopochtli – on the subjugated people. They constructed temples in the main plazas of tributary cities and in the spectacular mountain peaks, imposing the Aztec hummingbird god as supreme through the frescos, sculptures, and metalwork that now covered sites once dedicated to other gods.

They didn't just spread the worship of Huitzilopochtli; they also introduced other deities, such as their agricultural and nature gods. For instance, a relief of the water goddess Chalchiuhtlicue was commissioned to be erected near ancient Tula. Across the empire, artistic structures, carvings, and other Aztec artwork have been found, indicating the cultural influence of the Triple Cities over areas hundreds of miles away.

Aztec jaguar painting next to a mural of Annunciation in the cloister of the Franciscan monastery of Cuautinchan, built in the 1570s.[cii]

Even though the Aztec Empire was eventually conquered by the Spanish Empire, their art lived on - to a certain degree. The Amate paper continues to be produced today by Nahua artists from Guerrero. Franciscan and Austinian friars employed local Aztec artists to decorate their newly constructed churches in the decades following the Spanish conquest. Some Aztec murals have survived until today in churches in Mexico, such as a jaguar and eagle on each side of a mural of the annunciation in the Franciscan monastery of Cuautinchan in Pueblo.

Chapter 16: Aztec Mythology and Cosmology

Cosmology, from an anthropological perspective, is what gives the members of a specific culture a fundamental sense of identity. Cosmology is how a particular civilization perceives the universe: its beginnings and its ultimate destiny. It defines the place of a culture in the complexities of the cosmos, giving meaning to life and driving current actions.

So, what about the Aztecs? What was their cosmology? What did they believe about the origins of the universe? What was their sense of where they came from? How did they self-identify? What did they feel was their role in the cosmos? What did they believe was their ultimate destiny as a civilization?

Because the Aztecs freely borrowed from other cultures to build a cosmological hodgepodge, we will notice some inconsistencies in their myths. For instance, one myth says their hummingbird god, Huitzilopochtli, was the son of the creator god, Ometeotl, while another myth says he was the son of Coatlicue. Myths don't always fit neatly into the historical record.

In Aztec cosmology, the world consisted of three parts: the earth on which humans lived, an underworld called Mictlan (with nine layers), and the upper heavens or planes in the sky (with 13 layers). Humans could inhabit the earth and the underworld but could not penetrate the heavens, except for the lowest layer, and only certain people could do that. The lowest level of the heavens was a place of abundant water called Tlalocan, where the god, Tlaloc, lived.

The Aztecs believed that where a person went after dying depended on what they did in life but, more importantly, on how they died. The soul could go to one of four places: the land of the sun, the land of corn, the lowest heaven (Tlalocan), and the underworld Mictlan.

Mictlantecuhtli, god of the dead.[ciii]

Mictlan was not a fiery hell or a place of punishment. It was the place most people went after they died – but getting there wasn't easy. They had to go through an arduous journey and pass several trials along the way. When an Aztec person died, his or her loved ones would bury the body with helpful implements to assist them on their journey.

The eastern paradise of the sun was the destination of warriors who died in battle – all warriors, even the enemy warriors. Captured warriors who were sacrificed also went there. A person's soul would remain in the eastern paradise for four years; after that, they would be reincarnated as hummingbirds, eagles, owls, or butterflies, so they could return to earth to see how everything was going and to transmit subtle messages to those who listened.

Childbirth was considered a type of warfare, so if a woman died in the "war," she would go to the western paradise, the house of corn. She could return to the earth in a somewhat malevolent spirit form: the weeping woman of the night and the bringer of bad omens. The Aztecs believed these female spirits haunted crossroads and captured children there, so they would erect temples and leave food at crossroads so weeping women wouldn't kidnap their children.

The paradise of Tlalocan, the lowest level of heaven, was for people who drowned or were killed by lightning. It was also where people who died of leprosy and diseases associated with water went, along with the physically deformed. This afterworld had plenty of food. Interestingly, child sacrifice was often done by drowning; perhaps this was to ensure the babies would go to the paradise of Tlalocan.

In the highest heaven lived Ometecuhtli and Omecihuatl, the dual husband and wife creator gods, known collectively as Ometeotl. They were the dual god: two beings, yet one simultaneously. They were created out of nothing, and for a time, they were the only things that existed; nothing else had been created. Then, Ometeotl gave birth to four children: Xipe Totec (the flayed god), Tezcatlipoca (smoking mirror), Quetzalcoatl (feathered serpent), and Huitzilopochtli (hummingbird).

The *Myth of the Five Suns,* as recorded in the *Codex Chimalpopoca,* tells how the Aztec world came to be. Ometeotl gave the four children the task of creating a sun, a world, people to live in the world, and other gods. Quetzalcoatl and Huitzilopochtli were specifically given this task, but all the brothers were furiously competitive and kept creating drama (except for Xipe Totec, who seemed to stay on the sidelines). Each of the first four ages – earth, wind, fire, and water – ended in catastrophe. It took four attempts to create and sustain a world before they got everything right with the fifth attempt.

In the first creation, the *Age of the First Sun,* Quetzalcoatl and Huitzilopochtli created a sun. But it wasn't bright enough to give adequate light and heat. They then made the first man and first woman: Cipactonal and Oxomico. They were giants who ate acorns and were so strong they could uproot trees with their bare hands. Together, they had many children. The gods looked at their creation and decided it was not good. The sun was too weak.

Tezcatlipoca and Quetzalcoatl[iv]

So, Tezcatlipoca changed himself into the sun, which was bright enough and warm enough for the world. After 676 years, Tezcatlipoca's rival Quetzalcoatl was overwhelmed with jealousy that Tezcatlipoca was ruling as the sun. Quetzalcoatl took his club and knocked him out of the sky, and Tezcatlipoca plummeted into the ocean. In his rage at being knocked out of the sky, Tezcatlipoca emerged as a jaguar and ate all the giants, ending the age of the first sun.

In attempt number two, the age of the second sun, Quetzalcoatl took his place as the sun. He created (normal-sized) people who ate pine nuts. After 674 years, Tezcatlipoca took revenge against Quetzalcoatl. He came to the world in a blast of wind, so strong that it blew all the people away and even blew Quetzalcoatl the sun away. The few people who weren't blown away were changed into monkeys, and they ran off to the jungles to live.

In the third attempt, a new age began when Tlaloc, the god of rain, became the sun. This age lasted 364 years, and the people of this world ate the river reeds. In a fit of jealousy, Quetzalcoatl sent a rain of fire and burning stones, killing almost all mankind. Even the sun itself went up in flames. When the flames cooled, the ground was ashen, and the people who survived had become birds – turkeys, to be exact. Quetzalcoatl then gave the world to Tlaloc's wife, Chalchiuhtlicue, the *jade skirt woman.*

When Chalchiuhtlicue, the water goddess, took over the sun's responsibilities, the fourth age began. But she was the goddess of water, so it rained constantly. This age was the shortest, lasting for 312 years. Eventually, the great rain, so long and so hard, covered the earth with a flood that rose above the mountaintops; the people who survived became fish. Even the sun fell out of the sky, and then the sky fell down and covered the earth, so nothing could live on it.

The gods realized that fighting among themselves was counterproductive and that all the worlds they had made had been destroyed by their quarreling. Quetzalcoatl and Tezcatlipoca made peace with each other and went down to rebuild the world. They transformed themselves into great trees that pushed the sky back, dividing it from the earth below.

The gods all gathered around a bonfire in an attempt to create the fifth age – and to finally get it *right.* The gods knew that someone would have to sacrifice themselves to become the next sun for the new age. So, a handsome, strong (yet conceited) god, Tecuciztecatl, prepared himself to jump into the bonfire. Four times, he walked up to the fire, but each time he lost his nerve and walked away in shame.

Tonatiuh, god of the sun.[cv]

Finally, Nanahuatl, the smallest and humblest of the gods who was covered in leprosy, jumped into the flames. He became Tonatiuh, the sun; this was the birth of the fifth sun. Humiliated by Nanahuatl's sacrifice, Tecuciztecatl also leaped into the fire and became the moon. However, he was as bright as the sun, which the gods found inappropriate. One of the gods snatched a rabbit and threw it at him. When the rabbit hit the face of the moon, its light was dimmed. That is why the moon has the shape of a rabbit on its face.

Now they had a new problem. The sun was stuck. Tonatiuh, the god of the sun, told the other gods they would have to sacrifice themselves to get him moving. They jumped into the fire and became stars and planets, and finally, Tonatiuh could move across the sky. Because all the gods sacrificed themselves for the people of the earth, now people were expected to sacrifice themselves for the gods.

With the sun moving, Quetzalcoatl took on the task of creating new humans. He went to Mictlan to bring back the bones of the people who had died. Following a tense encounter with the god of the underworld, he took off running with the bag of bones and slipped and fell into a pit, breaking the bones. He eventually made it out and sprinkled his blood on the bones of the dead people, resurrecting them to life. Because they came from bone fragments, the men and women were all different sizes.

As mentioned previously, the Aztecs had two myths about their patron god Huitzilopochtli's birth. The first was probably borrowed from another culture, perhaps the Teotihuacan. The second one seemed to resonate more with the Aztecs, as they reenacted it annually at the Templo Mayor. The Aztecs traced their origins to the birth of Huitzilopochtli on their home island of Aztlan, on Mount Colhuacan (or Coatepec). In this version, Coatlicue (the scary goddess with the snake skirt) is Huitzilopochtli's mother. Coatlicue was sweeping her shrine one day when a ball of hummingbird feathers fell at her feet. She picked up the feathers and tucked them into her waistband, and this made her pregnant. Her other children (400 sons and her daughter, Coyolxauhqui) attacked her because of what they considered a dishonorable pregnancy. At that point, she gave birth to Huitzilopochtli, as mentioned in chapter 13, and he rose to her defense.

The Dominican friar and historian Diego Durán wrote an interesting account about the Aztec's origins in his 1581 book *Historia de las Indias de Nueva Espana* (known as the Durán Codex). Durán had come to Mexico at age seven with his family and became fluent in the Nahuatl language. After he became a priest, he spent much time among the local people, learning their customs and cosmology.

In his book, Durán recorded a story he had translated from an earlier Aztec history about Moctezuma I, the second Aztec Emperor, who ruled from 1440-1469, fifty years before the Spanish showed up. Moctezuma was curious about where their ancestors had lived and what those seven caves were like. He was fascinated by the tales of their ancestral island. Could they ever find it again?

Moctezuma sent for Cuauhcoatl, the royal historian, who told him that Aztlan had been a blissful, happy place whose name meant "whiteness." There was a great hill in the lake called Colhuacan, because it was twisted, and in this hill were caves and grottos of the Aztec ancestors. They lived in leisure, with all sorts of waterfowl – ducks, herons, cranes – at their disposal. They enjoyed the songs of the little birds with red and yellow heads in the groves of trees that grew on the island. Their ancestors got around the lake by canoe and planted floating gardens where they grew maize, chili, tomatoes, amaranth, and beans – which the Aztecs brought with them to the Valley of Mexico.

However, when they abandoned Aztlan and came to the mainland, the world turned against them. They struggled with biting weeds, sharp stones, brambles, and thorns that made it difficult to travel. They found no place to rest – the land was full of snakes, jaguars, and other dangerous creatures. The historian told Moctezuma I that this was what was painted in the ancient books.

Moctezuma organized an expedition to find Aztlan. His brother, Tlacaelel, cautioned him to carefully choose who would go along since this not a war campaign but a knowledge-gathering enterprise. Moctezuma gathered sixty sorcerers for a journey to find their mysterious homeland. They were to search out the place where their deity, Huitzilopochtli, was born and where his mother still lived. They carried with them treasures of gems, gold, vanilla, and cacao beans as gifts for their ancestors and the goddess.

The sorcerers succeeded in locating Aztlan. They arrived at the shores of a great lake, with a hill in the middle, and were delighted to hear the people speaking their own Nahuatl language. The local people carried them in their canoes to the island. At the bottom of the hill, they met an ancient man, the guardian-priest of the sanctuary of Coatlicue, the earth-mother goddess. He asked why they had come, and they told him they had been sent by their Emperor Moctezuma and his advisor Tlacaelel.

The old man frowned; he had never heard of those two men. But he did know the men who had left Aztlan centuries earlier. "Do you know them?" he asked, reciting the names of their ancestral leaders. "No," the sorcerers replied, "Those men all died long ago." The man looked at them, surprised. "But I was here when they left. All of us who saw them go are still alive now!"

The priest led them up the hill to meet the earth-mother goddess, Coatlicue. As they climbed the hill, the sorcerers began to sink into the sand. The priest looked at them quizzically. "What have you been eating?" They told them they had been drinking chocolate and eating the food grown in their new land." "That was your downfall," the priest said. "That's why your people die."

Coatlicue, mother of Huitzilopochtli[tvi]

Finally, they met the grotesque and filthy goddess, Coatlicue. She told them how she had been weeping ever since her son, Huitzilopochtli, had left. She said that she had not washed or changed her clothes or combed her hair since he had departed. She told them that Huitzilopochtli had left to guide the Aztecs (all seven tribes) on their long pilgrimage from Aztlan to the Valley of Mexico. Coatlicue longed for his promised return.

The goddess shared with them Huitzilopochtli's prophecy of the future he had told her before he left:

> "I must make war on all the provinces and cities and towns and places, taking them and subjecting them to my service. But in the same manner that I have conquered them, in this same manner they will be taken from me by conquering strangers, and I will be driven from that land. Then I will return to this place . . . then, mother, my time will be completed, and I will return fleeing to your lap."

The old man, the guardian of Coatlicue's sanctuary, told them the Aztecs had lost their immortality when they consumed rich foods and lusted for gold and other luxuries. He refused to accept the gifts the sorcerers brought but instead gave them gifts of plants and food from the island, where the people lived a simple but idyllic life. They also carried home a cloak made from the hemp of the maguey plant, a gift of the goddess for her sun Huitzilopochtli.

The sorcerers traveled home and related everything that happened to Moctezuma. The emperor broke into tears when he heard of the impending downfall of their empire. He took the maguey-fiber cloak to the temple of Huitzilopochtli. He fearfully consulted with his astrologers and prophets and with the ancient chronicles to identify the strangers who would one day come to conquer them.

In his account of the origins and history of the Aztecs, Friar Diego Durán stated three times that he copied *directly from the Aztec's own written history* as his primary source. The Aztec source document, called *Cronica X*, has been lost, but it served as a resource for other Spanish-language histories.

We can see that the cosmology of the Aztecs affected their beliefs about their role in war and sacrifice. An afterlife of the eastern paradise of the sun for fallen warriors and sacrificed victims would encourage the soldiers as they went to fight battles. It probably made the Aztecs (and their sacrificial victims) feel better about all the human sacrifices they were required to offer. The prophecies of Huitzilopochtli reinforced their mandate as conquerors of the surrounding lands.

But the prophecy also included dismal tidings of their future destiny – one day, they would be defeated by conquering strangers, and their god Huitzilopochtli would fly away from them and back to Aztlan and his mother. A similar prophecy had been given to Moctezuma I by Nezahualcoyotl, king of Texcoco. Moctezuma II had received a prophecy from Nezahualcoyotl's son, Nezahualpilli, that foreigners would overcome the empire. Perhaps this is why Moctezuma II, great-grandson of Moctezuma I, chose not to confront the Spanish conquistadors in an all-out battle, fatalistically submitting to the prophecies.

Conclusion

Before the Aztecs grew into a mighty empire, they lived a simple, unassuming life somewhere northwest of the Valley of Mexico. Whether as fishers and farmers on the idyllic island of Aztlan or simply as Chichimeca hunters and gatherers, they probably had no inkling of the destiny that would one day be theirs.

Without the wheel and without a fully developed alphabet, they emerged from humble beginnings to build a highly organized city of 200,000 people on a swampy island, the largest city in the Americas and one of the largest in the world at the time. They constructed huge temples and pyramids and conquered and ruled an area of 80,000 square miles with up to six million people.

Great civilizations had risen and fallen before these wandering nomads drifted into Central Mexico. These civilizations influenced the Aztecs, masters of assimilation and adaptation, and thus the Aztecs became preservers of these exceptional cultures. The Olmec built the first true cities and the first pyramids of Mesoamerica and carved 11-foot-high colossal heads weighing several tons, which they somehow transported 50 miles to their cities. The transitional culture of the Epi-Olmec developed a sophisticated calendar and writing system at least as early as 32 BC.

Then the mighty Toltec civilization, admired and emulated by the Aztecs, rose to preeminence from their Nahuatl-speaking Chichimeca origins. Fierce Toltec warriors extended their empire from the Pacific to the Gulf, penetrating the Yucatan Peninsula as they spread the Cult of Quetzalcoatl. They built the astonishing 15-foot-high Atlantes of Tula columns to support their massive porticoes, and their famed artisans produced beautiful carvings, artwork, and jewelry.

An unknown force impelled the Mexica and the other Aztec tribes to leave their blissful Aztlan homeland – perhaps a natural disaster, perhaps an internal struggle, or perhaps domination by another culture. For over 100 years, they wandered through a land turned against them – deserts of thorns, sharp rocks, snakes, and poisonous lizards – until they reached the fertile Valley of Mexico. They encountered their kinsmen from Aztlan there, but their fellow Aztecs were unwelcoming, unwilling to compete for the land, resources, and power for which they were striving.

While hiding among the reeds from the Colhuacan army, they received a prophecy from their hummingbird god, Huitzilopochtli: in the morning, they were to search for a prickly-pear cactus among the reeds on which an eagle would be perched. This was where they were to build their city, Tenochtitlan, and then they were to conquer their surrounding enemies, all of them, one by one. After years of wandering, fighting the elements, and struggling to survive, they found the eagle on the cactus, on an island in the lake. They had a place to call home. The next part of the prophecy was an extended military campaign of subjugating provinces and cities.

First, they had to build their city, form important alliances, and grow in strength. Finally, they reached the point where they formed a coalition with other city-states victimized by the despotic demands of their overlords, the Tepanec city-state of Azcapotzalco. After overthrowing Azcapotzalco, the three Aztec tribes – the Mexica of Tenochtitlan, the Acolhua of Texcoco, and the Tepanec of

Tlacopan – formed the Triple Alliance. This became the Aztec Empire, with a self-identity as the chosen people called by the god Huitzilopochtli to conquer and rule over other lands.

For almost 200 years, the extraordinary Aztec Empire ruled the Valley of Mexico, expanding to dominate a substantial part of Mesoamerica. They developed a civilization renown for military conquest, extensive market exchange, fascinating culture, and sophisticated agricultural endeavors. They flourished as an intricate religious, political, social, and trade organization of over 500 city-states.

Their downfall came not only because of the Spaniard's superior military technology (calvary, crossbows, cannons) but also the unrest among tributary cultures and the ongoing warfare with non-Aztec civilizations on the outskirts of their civilization. Their tributary provinces were disgruntled regarding high tribute payments with few benefits. Their own city-states and the Aztec's Tlaxcala rivals grieved their children taken as slaves and sacrifices. The Aztecs failed to learn from their own history – the reason they formed an alliance to overthrow the Azcapotzalco Empire was because of the Tepanec cruelty and despotic demands. Now, the Tlaxcala threw in their lot with the Spaniards, and even the Cholula and other allies betrayed them, forming an army of 150,00 indigenous people that marched against the Aztec Empire with the conquistadors.

An ancient proverb says, "Know well the condition of your flocks." The Aztec style of leadership generated animosity and resentment, influencing their flocks to stray. They harshly ruled their provinces through terror rather than in a more harmonious collaboration – as the Purépecha-Tarascan did. Leadership is stewardship; it's actively preparing for the future vitality of one's organization, community, or nation. This is where the Aztecs failed.

The Aztecs constantly attacked and antagonized their undefeated enemies, the Tlaxcala, creating murderous hatred that came back to haunt them. In our society and in our world today, it's better to negotiate a truce with our most intransigent adversaries because one day, we might need them as allies. Antagonism is counterproductive to any endeavor and has doomed many leaders, even in the present day.

How have the Aztecs influenced and inspired the current citizens of Mexico and Central America? Yes. The Aztec economy helped shape the economic structure of modern-day Mexico City. The city of Tenochtitlan had several guilds of skilled craftsmen, but they lacked raw materials. Thus, the Aztecs created an economic exchange of commodities, capital, and assets through tribute, local and long-distance trade, and market transactions, which influenced methods of trade in today's Mexico City.

Ulama.[cvii]

Much of the everyday culture of the Aztecs pervades the culture of Mexico and Central America, and even the United States. Mexicans still have a diet based on the Aztec core foods: corn, beans, tortillas, tomatoes, guacamole, and chilis, all of which are enjoyed not only in today's Mexico, but also throughout North America. And let's not forget chocolate, loved around the world! Ulama was a favorite ball game of the Aztecs. This game is still played today throughout Mesoamerica. Ulama has some similarities to Mexico's favorite sport of soccer (association football), igniting great passion in communities and as a nation.

Indigenous ladies in Cuetzalan, Puebla, Mexico, wearing huipil clothing. The lady on the left is wearing huarache sandals.[cviii]

Clothing in Central America and Mexico has origins in Aztec culture. The *cactli* and *huarache* sandals the nobility wore have endured as common footwear and even fashion statements throughout Mexico, Central America, and even around the world. The loose-fitting *huipil* (or *huanengo*) clothing of Aztec ladies is still the favored garment of the indigenous women in Mexico and Central America.

Traditional music, dances, and Aztec artwork are displayed at important festivals. The Nahuatl language has survived, and 1.7 indigenous people in Mexico speak dialects of the ancient language, mostly in the rural areas surrounding Mexico City. One-third of the Nahua people only speak the Nahua language and not Spanish. The Nahua people, ethnically related to the Aztecs and Toltecs, are the largest indigenous people group in Mexico and also live in El Salvador, Honduras, and Nicaragua.

Aztec dance/ritual at Juana de Asbaje Park in Tlalpan, Mexico City.[cix]

An interesting vestige of Aztec society was the *pepenilia* – or street scavengers. The people of Tenochtitlan were committed to cleanliness, and the pepenilia were responsible for recovering recyclable items. Today, Mexico City has troops of *pepenadores* who scour the streets for items they can scavenge. The Spanish word *pepenadores* stems from the Nahuatl word, which means to choose or select.

The Aztecs developed (or improved on) numerous achievements in civilization simultaneously but independently of similar achievements in Europe, Africa, and Asia. They used the *chinampas* form of agriculture, a 365-day calendar, and remarkable step pyramids. They implemented advanced city planning and built aqueducts for fresh drinking water in Tenochtitlan. They had a strong sense of order and used a merit system that rewarded hard work and innovation. They had mandatory education for all teens, regardless of class or gender. They had a well-developed justice system, and nobility, who were regarded as role models, were punished more strictly than commoners.

They had a number system, and utilized multiplication, division, and geometry in their trade, in their impressive architecture, and in craftwork. They used algorithms to calculate area. Without knowing the size of the earth, they figured out when eclipses would happen. They kept organized and detailed documents of tribute payments and trade transactions.

When the Spaniards entered Tenochtitlan, they were impressed with its size and its orderliness. They commented on the cleanliness of the people and the pristine streets of the great city. Remember, this was a city of 200,000 people, built over water. They depended on the fish, frogs, ducks, and other water animals for food, so if they polluted the water, they might lose a valuable food source. They relied on a remarkable waste management system to keep Lake Texcoco and their city reasonably clean.

Human excrement and organic waste were recycled as fertilizer for the chinampas. Urine was recycled as a fixative in fabric dying. At night, public areas were lit by burnable trash, which also provided fuel for cooking and warmth in the homes. Dropping litter or dumping human waste on the streets was punishable by law. They understood the importance of trees; cutting one down without permission could generate the death penalty. They recycled whatever they could in a culture that was resource-efficient and minimized waste, serving as a model for cities today.

The Aztecs were culturally and mentally connected to other great Mesoamerican civilizations – such as the Mayas, Toltecs, and Olmecs – through the great significance their religion and their gods played in their lives. They were all polytheistic and shared several of the same deities. They valued hard work, worship, and warfare as their greatest priorities, reflected in their architecture, artwork, sculptures, and paintings.

The legacy of the Aztecs, and specifically the Mexica tribe, lives on in the name of the country and capital city of Mexico and of its people. When the Spaniards arrived, the Mexica city-states of the Triple Alliance were called Mexico-Tenochtitlan. Following the Spanish conquest, they called the city they built over the ruins of Tenochtitlan *La Ciudad de Mexico.* After gaining independence from Spain, the country's official name is the *Estados Unidos Mexicanos* (United Mexican States), but it is more commonly called Mexico.

Flag of Mexico[cx]

The flag of Mexico has its coat of arms in the center – the same overall design that has been used since independence from Spain in 1821. The Mexican coat of arms is based on the Aztec pictograph for Tenochtitlan, featuring an eagle with a snake in its claw, perched on a prickly pear cactus on a rock rising out of a lake.

After tracing the rise and fall of the Aztec Empire, what deductions can we make? When gauging the importance of their history in today's contemporary society, we can consider their strengths and their weaknesses. A compelling key to their success was their canny ability to form brilliant alliances. This skill can certainly be put into play in today's organizations, economic endeavors, and politics. The Aztecs were also empowered by vision – a strong sense of who they were and what they were meant to do. A robust self-identity and grasp of a distinct destiny will impel individuals, corporations, and nations to greatness. A third strength was their willingness to learn from other cultures, absorbing their technologies, craftsmanship, and knowledge. When we are willing to learn from other people and other cultures, it opens doors, keeps us relevant, and increases our adaptability and chances of success.

Free limited time bonus

Stop for a moment. We have a free bonus set up for you. The problem is this: we forget 90% of everything that we read after 7 days. Crazy fact, right? Here's the solution: we've created a printable, 1-page pdf summary for this book that you're reading now. All you have to do to get your free pdf summary is to go to the following website:

https://livetolearn.lpages.co/enthrallinghistory/

Once you do, it will be intuitive. Enjoy, and thank you!

We forget 90% of everything that we've read in 7 days...

Get the free printable pdf summary of the book you've read AND much, much more... shhhh...

Enter Your Most Frequently Used Email to Get Started

DOWNLOAD FREE PDF SUMMARY

© Enthralling History

Bibliography

Bellamy, Kate. "On the External Relations of Purepecha: An Investigation into Classification, Contact and Patterns of Word Formation." Doctoral Theses, University of Leiden, 2018, https://www.lotpublications.nl/Documents/498_fulltext.pdf.

Berdan, Frances. *Aztecs of Central Mexico: An Imperial Society.* Belmont, CA, USA: Cengage Learning, April 28, 2004.

Bierhorst, John. *History and Mythology of the Aztecs: The Codex Chimalpopoca.* University of Arizona Press, June 1, 1998.

Blanton, Richard. "Prehispanic Settlement Patterns of the Ixtapalapa Peninsula Region, Mexico." PhD diss., University of Michigan, 1970.

Blanton, Richard. "Prehispanic Adaptation in the Ixtapalapa Region, Mexico." *Science,* 175 (4028) (1972):1317-26.

Burkhart, Louise M. "The Solar Christ in Nahuatl Doctrinal Texts of Early Colonial Mexico." *Ethnohistory,* 35, no. 3 (1988): 234-56. Accessed June 10, 2021. doi:10.2307/481801.

Carrasco, Pedro. *The Tenochca Empire of Ancient Mexico: The Triple Alliance of Tenochtitlan, Tetzcoco, and Tlacopan.* University of Oklahoma Press, March 1, 2011.

Clendinnen, Inga. *Aztecs: An Interpretation.* Cambridge University Press, July 28, 2014.

Coe, Michael D., Javier Urcid, Rex Koontz. *Mexico: From the Olmecs to the Aztecs.* Thames & Hudson, September 17, 2019.

Colston, Stephen A. "'No Longer Will There Be a Mexico:' Omens, Prophecies, and the Conquest of the Aztec Empire." *American Indian Quarterly,* 9, no. 3 (1985): 239-58. Accessed June 1, 2021. doi:10.2307/1183828.

Cortés, Hernán. *Cartas y Relaciones de* Hernán *Cortés al Emperador Carlos V.* Edited by Pascual de Gayangos. Paris: A. Chaix, 1866. Microfilm.

Cruz, Isabel De La, Angélica González-Oliver, Brian M. Kemp, Juan A. Román, David Glenn Smith, and Alfonso Torre-Blanco. "Sex Identification of Children Sacrificed to the Ancient Aztec Rain Gods in Tlatelolco." *Current Anthropology* 49, no. 3 (2008): 519-26. Accessed June 10, 2021. doi:10.1086/587642.

Dewan, Leslie and Hosler, Dorothy. "Ancient Maritime Trade on Balsa Rafts: An Engineering Analysis." *Journal of Archaeological Research,* Vol. 64 (2008): 19-36.

Elzey, Wayne. "A Hill on a Land Surrounded by Water: An Aztec Story of Origin and Destiny." *History of Religions,* 31, no. 2 (1991):105-49. Accessed June 16, 2021. http://www.jstor.org/stable/1063021.

Hosler, Dorothy. "West Mexican Metallurgy: South and Central American Origins and West Mexican Transformations." *American Anthropologist,* Vol. 90, No. 4 (1988): 832-843.

Ioannidis, Alexander G., Javier Blanco-Portillo, and Andres Moreno-Estrada. "Native American Gene Flow into Polynesia Predating Easter Island Settlement." *Nature,* Vol. 583 (2020): 572-77.

Levy, Buddy. *Conquistador: Hernan Cortes, King Montezuma, and the Last Stand of the Aztecs.* New York: Bantam, July 28, 2009.

Lockhart, James. *The Nahuas after the Conquest: A Social and Cultural History of the Indians of Central Mexico, Sixteenth Through Eighteenth Centuries.* Stanford University Press, September 1, 1994.

Matthew, Laura E., Michel R. Oudijk. *Indian Conquistadors: Indigenous Allies in the Conquest of Mesoamerica.* University of Oklahoma Press, October 22, 2012.

Miller, Mary Ellen. *The Art of Mesoamerica: From Olmec to Aztec (World of Art).*Thames & Hudson, June 11, 2019.

Pohl, John, Adam Hook. *Aztecs and Conquistadores: The Spanish Invasion and the Collapse of the Aztec Empire.* Osprey Publishing, October 10, 2005.

Powis TG, A. Cyphers, N. W. Gaikwad, L. Grivetti, and K. Cheong. "Cacao Use and the San Lorenzo Olmec." *Proceedings of the National Academy of Sciences,* 108(21)(2011): 8595-600.

Smith, Michael E. *The Aztecs, 3rd Edition.* Wiley.com, December 27, 2011.

Strawn, Susan M., "Hand Spinning and Cotton in the Aztec Empire, as Revealed by the Codex Mendoza." *Textile Society of America Symposium Proceedings.* 5 (2002).

Thomas, Hugh. *Conquest: Cortes, Montezuma, and the Fall of Old Mexico.* Simon & Schuster, April 7, 1995.

Valentini, Philipp J. T. "The Olmecas and the Tultecas: A Study in Early Mexican Ethnology and History." *American Antiquarian Society,* (October 1882): pp. 209-30, https://www.americanantiquarian.org/proceedings/48003300.pdf.

ⁱ https://www.needpix.com/photo/892953/aztec-calendar-aztec

ⁱⁱ https://en.wikipedia.org/wiki/Aztecs#Mexica_migration_and_foundation_of_Tenochtitlan

iii https://en.wikipedia.org/wiki/Olmecs#/media/File:Olmec_Heartland_Overview_4.svg

iv https://commons.wikimedia.org/wiki/File:Altar_4_La_Venta_(Ruben_Charles).jpg

v http://www.quantumgaze.com/curious/olmec-great-pyramid-la-venta/

vi https://www.needpix.com/photo/download/304570/olmec-head-tabasco-sale-mexico-mesoamerica-free-pictures-free-photos-free-images

vii https://commons.wikimedia.org/wiki/File:Olmec_Figurine_holding_infant_(Met).jpg

viii https://en.wikipedia.org/wiki/Werejaguar#/media/File:Jaguarbaby.jpg

ix Source: Audrey and George Delange
https://commons.wikimedia.org/wiki/File:La_Venta_Stele_19_(Delange).jpg

x *From the Museum of Anthropology at Xalapa, Vera Cruz, Mexico.*
https://en.wikipedia.org/wiki/Epi-Olmec_culture#/media/File:Harvestermountainlord.jpg

xi Leandro Neumann Ciuffo from Rio de Janeiro, Brazil - Pirâmide Tolteca de Tula
https://en.wikipedia.org/wiki/Toltec#/media/File:Piramide_tolteca_de_Tula_(1).jpg

xii https://commons.wikimedia.org/wiki/File:Toltec_influence_cities_marked1.jpg

xiii https://commons.wikimedia.org/wiki/File:Topiltzin.jpg

xiv https://commons.wikimedia.org/wiki/File:El_descubrimiento_del_pulque_Jos%C3%A9_Mar%C3%ADa_Obreg%C3%B3n.jpg

xv Gary Todd https://commons.wikimedia.org/wiki/File:Toltec_Chac_Mool.jpg

xvi Cangadoba. https://commons.wikimedia.org/wiki/File:Quetzalcoatl_isolated.png

xvii Alejandro Linares Garcia https://commons.wikimedia.org/wiki/File:TulaSite81.JPG

xviii Daniel Schwen. https://commons.wikimedia.org/wiki/File:Chichen_Itza_2.jpg

xix https://commons.wikimedia.org/wiki/File:Mapa_de_San_Miguel_y_San_Felipe_de_los_Chichimecas_(1580)_-_Chichimecas_2.jpg

xx https://commons.wikimedia.org/wiki/File:Baj%C3%ADo_Mx.png

xxi https://commons.wikimedia.org/wiki/File:ChichimecNations.png

xxii https://commons.wikimedia.org/wiki/File:Centro_Ceremonial_Chichimeca.jpg

xxiii https://commons.wikimedia.org/wiki/File:Mapa_de_San_Miguel_y_San_Felipe_de_los_Chichimecas_(1580)_-_Chichimecas_1.jpg

xxiv https://commons.wikimedia.org/wiki/File:San_Felipe,_Guanajuato_-_Mapa_de_San_Miguel_y_San_Felipe_de_los_Chichimecas_(1580).jpg

xxv https://commons.wikimedia.org/wiki/File:Codex_Boturini,_page_3.jpg

xxvi https://commons.wikimedia.org/wiki/File:Tenoch.jpg

xxvii https://commons.wikimedia.org/wiki/File:MA_D037_From_the_Boturini_MS_showing_the_commencement_of_the_Aztec_migration.jpg

xxviii https://commons.wikimedia.org/wiki/File:ToltecaChichimeca_Chicomostoc.jpg

xxix https://commons.wikimedia.org/wiki/File:LA_QUEMADA_zacatecas.jpg

xxx https://commons.wikimedia.org/wiki/File:Ruinas,_La_Quemada_-_panoramio_(4).jpg

xxxi https://commons.wikimedia.org/wiki/File:1704_Gemelli_Map_of_the_Aztec_Migration_from_Aztlan_to_Chapultapec_-_Geographicus_-_AztecMigration-gemelli-1704.jpg

xxxii https://commons.wikimedia.org/wiki/File:Boturini_Codex_(folio_3).JPG

xxxiii https://commons.wikimedia.org/wiki/File:Boturini_Codex_(folio_4).JPG

xxxiv https://commons.wikimedia.org/wiki/File:Basin_of_Mexico_1519_map-en.svg

xxxv https://commons.wikimedia.org/wiki/File:Codice_Aubin_Folio_25.png

xxxvi https://commons.wikimedia.org/wiki/File:The_Eagle,_the_Snake,_and_the_Cactus_in_the_Founding_of_Tenochtitlan_WDL6749.png

xxxvii https://commons.wikimedia.org/wiki/File:Acamapichtli,_the_First_Aztec_King_(Reigned_1376%E2%80%9395)_WDL6718.png

xxxviii https://commons.wikimedia.org/wiki/File:Historia_general_de_las_cosas_de_Nueva_Espa%C3%B1a_vol._1_folio_74v_(cleared_up).png

xxxix https://commons.wikimedia.org/wiki/File:El_templo_mayor_en_Tenochtitlan.png

xl https://commons.wikimedia.org/wiki/File:The_American_Museum_journal_(c1900-(1918))_(18162300141).jpg

xli https://commons.wikimedia.org/wiki/File:Tezozomoc_funeral.jpg

xlii https://commons.wikimedia.org/wiki/File:Four_Aztec_Warriors_in_Drawn_in_Codex_Mendoza.jpg

xliii https://commons.wikimedia.org/wiki/File:Aztecexpansion.png

xliv https://commons.wikimedia.org/wiki/File:Nezahualcoyotl.jpg

xlv https://commons.wikimedia.org/wiki/File:The_Battle_of_Azcapotzalco_WDL6746.png

xlvi https://commons.wikimedia.org/wiki/File:Aztec_Empire_1519_map-es.svg

xlvii https://commons.wikimedia.org/wiki/File:Aztec_warriors.png

xlviii https://commons.wikimedia.org/wiki/File:Ba%C3%B1os_de_Nezahualcoyotl.JPG

xlix https://commons.wikimedia.org/wiki/File:Moctezuma_I,_the_Fifth_Aztec_King.png

l https://commons.wikimedia.org/wiki/File:PatzcuaroLakeIslands_fromTheTopOfJanitzioIsland_PatzcuaroLake_MichoacanMexico.jpg

li https://en.wikipedia.org/wiki/Pre-Columbian_rafts#/media/File:Andean_raft,_1748.jpg

lii https://en.wikipedia.org/wiki/Tarascan_state#/media/File:Tarascan_Coyote_Statuette.jpg

liii https://upload.wikimedia.org/wikipedia/commons/e/e4/4thYacatatztztz.JPG

liv https://commons.wikimedia.org/wiki/File:Tarascan_aztec_states.png

lv By Thelmadatter - Own work, CC BY-SA 3.0, https://commons.wikimedia.org/w/index.php?curid=8481277

^{lvi} https://commons.wikimedia.org/wiki/File:Ornamenta_Pur%C3%A9pecha.jpg

^{lvii} *https://en.wikipedia.org/wiki/Michoac%C3%A1n#/media/File:Aztec_Indians_Mexico_Tl axcalan_Cortez.jpg*

^{lviii} https://commons.wikimedia.org/wiki/File:Moctezuma_Xocoyotzin_Newberry.jpg

^{lix}https://en.wikipedia.org/wiki/Juan_de_Grijalva#/media/File:Expedici%C3%B3n_de_Girja lva_1518.svg

^{lx} https://commons.wikimedia.org/wiki/File:Cortes_hernan_2.jpg

^{lxi}https://en.wikipedia.org/wiki/La_Malinche#/media/File:MOM_D093_Donna_Marina_(L a_Malinche).jpg

^{lxii} https://upload.wikimedia.org/wikipedia/commons/7/7f/Cempoala_location_map-fr.svg

^{lxiii} *http://bancroft.berkeley.edu/Exhibits/nativeamericans/lg25_1.html, Public Domain, https://commons.wikimedia.org/w/index.php?curid=5801517*

^{lxiv}*https://commons.wikimedia.org/wiki/File:Cortez_and_Montezuma_at_Mexican_Temple. jpg*

^{lxv}https://commons.wikimedia.org/wiki/File:Los_informantes_de_moctezuma_Isidro_Mart %C3%ADnez_siglo_XIX.jpg

^{lxvi} *By Jl FilpoC - Own work, CC BY-SA 4.0, https://commons.wikimedia.org/w/index.php?curid=79340037*

^{lxvii} https://commons.wikimedia.org/wiki/File:Stories_of_American_explorers_-_a_historical_reader_(1906)_(14592623230).jpg

^{lxviii}*https://commons.wikimedia.org/wiki/File:ROHM_D273_Aztecs_continue_their_assault _against_the_conquistadors.jpg*

^{lxix} https://commons.wikimedia.org/wiki/File:Manuel_Rodriguez_de_Guzman_-_Battle_of_Otumba_-_1983.591_-_Museum_of_Fine_Arts.jpg

^{lxx} https://www.pinclipart.com/pindetail/iixxx_brigantine-line-art-drawing-ship-carrack-hernan-cortes/

^{lxxi} https://commons.wikimedia.org/wiki/File:Basin_of_Mexico_1519_map-fr.svg

^{lxxii} https://commons.wikimedia.org/wiki/File:The_Conquest_of_Tenochtitlan.jpg

^{lxxiii}https://commons.wikimedia.org/wiki/File:ROHM_D201_The_conquistadors_enter_ten ochtitlan_to_the_sounds_of_martial_music.jpg

^{lxxiv} http://www.munal.com.mx, Public Domain, https://commons.wikimedia.org/w/index.php?curid=21809420

^{lxxv} By Jaontiveros - Own work, CC BY-SA 4.0, https://commons.wikimedia.org/w/index.php?curid=6222300

^{lxxvi} https://commons.wikimedia.org/wiki/File:Templo_Mayor_50.jpg

^{lxxvii} https://commons.wikimedia.org/wiki/File:Misi%C3%B3n_Santiago_de_Jalpan.jpg

lxxviii https://commons.wikimedia.org/wiki/File:Bernardino_de_Sahag%C3%BAn.jpg

lxxix https://commons.wikimedia.org/wiki/File:Blowing_on_maize.jpg

lxxx https://commons.wikimedia.org/wiki/File:Mestizo._Mestiza._Mestiza.jpg

lxxxi https://commons.wikimedia.org/wiki/File:Guide_leaflet_(1901)_(14581791148).jpg

lxxxii https://commons.wikimedia.org/wiki/File:Templo_Mayor_2015_007.jpg

lxxxiii https://commons.wikimedia.org/wiki/File:General_guide_to_the_exhibition_halls_of_th e_American_Museum_of_Natural_History_(1911)_(14595489267).jpg

lxxxiv https://commons.wikimedia.org/wiki/File:COM_V2_D273_Prisoners_for_sacrifice_wer e_decorated.png

lxxxv https://en.wikipedia.org/wiki/Human_sacrifice_in_Aztec_culture#/media/File:20041229-Ocelotl-Cuauhxicalli_(Museo_Nacional_de_Antropolog%C3%ADa)_MQ.jpg

lxxxvi https://commons.wikimedia.org/wiki/File:TemploMayor4.jpg

lxxxvii https://commons.wikimedia.org/wiki/File:Danzantes_Bas%C3%ADlica_de_Guadalupe.j pg

lxxxviii https://commons.wikimedia.org/wiki/File:Irrigaci%C3%B3n_con_uictli_C%C3%B3dice _Florentino_libro_XI_f.228.jpg.

lxxxix https://commons.wikimedia.org/wiki/File:Murales_Rivera_-_Markt_in_Tlatelolco_1.jpg

xc https://commons.wikimedia.org/wiki/File:Aztec_high_lords_bottom.png

xci https://commons.wikimedia.org/wiki/File:Bodl_Arch.Selden.A.1_roll236.2_frame5.jpg

xcii https://commons.wikimedia.org/w/index.php?search=Aztec+board+game&title=Special: MediaSearch&go=Go&type=image

xciii https://commons.wikimedia.org/wiki/File:Cacao_-_Fig_1._Aztec_glyph_or_pictograph_for_80_bales_of_cacao.png

xciv https://commons.wikimedia.org/wiki/File:Aztec_Sun_Stone_Replica_cropped.jpg

xcv https://commons.wikimedia.org/wiki/File:Cuauhxicalli_de_Moctezuma_Ilhuicamina.JPG

xcvi https://commons.wikimedia.org/wiki/File:Diosa_Coatlicue.jpg

xcvii https://commons.wikimedia.org/wiki/File:Xipe_Totec_Annotation.jpg

xcviii https://commons.wikimedia.org/wiki/File:Central_Mexico,_Aztec,_13th-16th_century_-_Goddess_Plaque_-_1949.199_-_Cleveland_Museum_of_Art.tif

xcix https://commons.wikimedia.org/wiki/File:Double_headed_turquoise_serpentAztecbritish _museum.jpg

c https://commons.wikimedia.org/wiki/File:Mesoamerica,_puebla,_cholula,_mixteca-puebla_(nahua-mixteca),_ciotola_con_piede,_1200-1521_ca._02.jpg

ci https://commons.wikimedia.org/wiki/File:Feather_headdress_Moctezuma_II.JPG

cii https://commons.wikimedia.org/wiki/File:Cuautinchan7.JPG

[ciii] https://commons.wikimedia.org/wiki/File:Mictlantecuhtli-retouched.jpg

[civ] https://commons.wikimedia.org/wiki/File:Quetzalcoatl_and_Tezcatlipoca.jpg

[cv] https://commons.wikimedia.org/wiki/File:Mexico_-_Museo_de_antropologia_-_Tonatiuh_en_jarre_rouge.JPG

[cvi] https://commons.wikimedia.org/wiki/File:2013-12-24_Coatlicue_anagoria.JPG

[cvii] https://commons.wikimedia.org/wiki/File:Ulama_37_(Aguilar).jpg

[cviii] https://commons.wikimedia.org/wiki/File:Indigenous_women_market.jpg

[cix] https://commons.wikimedia.org/wiki/File:AztecDanceRitualAsbaje08.jpg

[cx] https://commons.wikimedia.org/wiki/File:Flag_of_Mexico.jpg